FLORAL

CONTEMPORARY

OLIVIER
DUPON

FLORAL
CONTEMPORARY

THE RENAISSANCE
IN FLOWER DESIGN

Thames & Hudson

WITH 342 ILLUSTRATIONS,
339 IN COLOUR

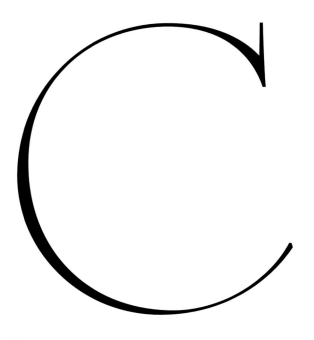

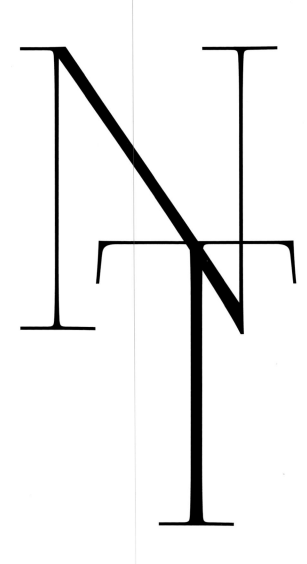

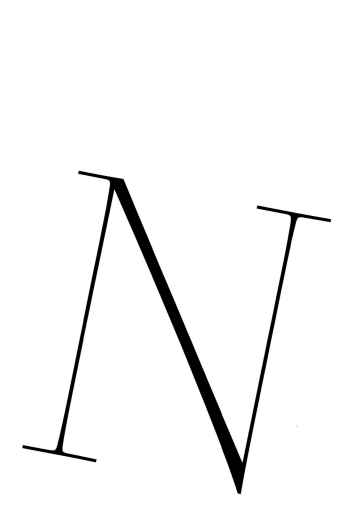
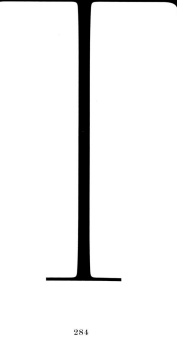
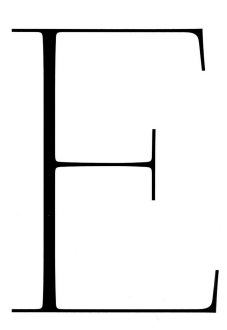

INTRODUCTION

WE ALL ASSOCIATE FLOWERS WITH
IMPORTANT OCCASIONS, WHETHER
CELEBRATORY OR COMMEMORATIVE,
BUT WE SHOULD ALSO EMBRACE THEM
ROUTINELY, IF ONLY TO BETTER OUR LIVES.
FLORAL STILL LIFES CAN RAVISH OUR
SENSES AND REFLECT EVERY MOOD.

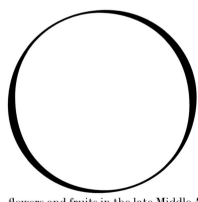 f all the fascinating trades that have long been prac-
tised, floristry must count as among the most special.
I remember being enraptured by the sumptuous
array presented in Jan Brueghel the Younger's
A Basket of Flowers, an oil on wood painting at the
Metropolitan Museum of Art in New York. Witnessing,
among other things, the current renaissance of the
Old World touch – young florists seeking out heirloom varietals and designing with a Dutch master's
flair – is therefore a particular joy. We may have
lost the significance of the iconography of flowers in
today's arrangements, so prevalent in still lifes of
flowers and fruits in the late Middle Ages, but what we have gained is limitless artistry.

I believe the English language captures the essence correctly when it speaks of 'still life',
whereas the French *nature morte* (dead nature) could not be more anomalous for a pictorial
celebration of life. Painted blooms will remain forever fresh, unlike cut flowers whose ephemerality is a certainty – a necessary reminder that one should seek solace in the present. Who
can resist the inherent beauty of flora? It is confirmation that nature is perfect. The great
testimony lies in the fact that flowers are almost the only things that remain beautiful – if
embracing a different version of their beauty – in death.

Just a glance through these pages confirms that real floral art is a serious endeavour,
not merely 'puff and fluff' and not something to be stereotyped as 'feminine'. Long hours,
physical hardship and low retail margins are often the florist's lot. But is there anything more
noble and honourable than crafting with a living material?

While working on this book, it has been heart-
ening to witness the effort an increasing number of
floral artists have been making to source their stock
responsibly, thereby sustaining allotment holders
and local flower growers. Some florists even manage
their own flower farms. Most flowers, however, are
still extensively cultivated miles away from where
they are sold. Although this means a great source of
revenue for the country of origin, it is important to
strike a balance for the protection of our planet. So
when the time comes to plan a wedding or a party,
it may be an idea to insist on having seasonal flowers that are sourced from nearby growers.

Another realization has been that – beyond
ingrained national traits and, conversely, a certain
uniform way of styling flowers across the world – a
few trends have crossed borders, proponents inter-
preting them with their own touch. Even more
beguiling has been the discovery of talents who are
forging their own path and working with flowers in
totally unique ways, irrespective of trends.

This book has been conceived from the floral
artists' perspective, as homage to their inspirational works. You will not find any methodological
tips on how to make an arrangement, nor ency-
clopedic information on types of flowers. This is
first and foremost a showcase for some of today's
great floral makers, confirming that contemporary
floral art comes in all shapes and guises, whether
carried out by traditionalists, aficionados of the
rustic style, or conceptual artists. What unites the
makers is that each is committed to a new kind of
poetic scripture, and every one of their works is a
stunning, living sculpture.

Working on this book has had a marked effect
on me. Once a week I now rush to the best local
flower shop, engage with the florist, ask the names
of flowers and experiment with how the blooms
work together. I defy you not to feel the same urge.

ALEKSANDRA SCHUTZ

AUSTRALIA

"EVERY PROJECT, REGARDLESS OF SIZE OR COMPLEXITY, DEEPENS MY LOVE OF FLOWERS, AND NOTHING EXCITES ME MORE THAN SEEING HOW I CAN HELP SET A MOOD BY RESPONDING TO NATURE'S BEAUTY. IN THE FUTURE I'D LIKE TO EXPERIMENT WITH PLANTS THAT ARE ALIEN TO ME, AND SEE WHAT EFFECT THAT HAS ON MY CREATIVITY."

When family history and an exotic heritage collide, it can lay the foundation for a life that sounds pre-destined. Aleksandra Schutz's family migrated from Latvia to Australia, where they initially settled on farms, growing carnations, dahlias and tomatoes. "We always celebrated Latvian festivals. At Midsummer Solstice we would wear national costume and handmade flower crowns, and decorate the hall with oak leaves," recalls Aleksandra. "My parents also owned a wholesale nursery. As kids, we'd run through the potted gardenias and grevilleas, and enjoy the beautiful smell of jasmine in summer. Every Sunday our grandparents would visit with armfuls of flowers picked from their garden, and on birthdays they would bring *klingeris*, the traditional Latvian birthday cake, decorated with camellias." Despite all this, working with flowers never crossed Aleksandra's mind. Instead she took a job at the Dinosaur Design homewares and jewelry studio. "Assisting there provided a great hands-on masterclass. Their work is incredibly sensual and tactile, which I relate to. I spent many an hour arranging products, experimenting with colour combinations, shapes, surfaces and textures." Years later a friend introduced her to the art of ikebana. After that she joined Grandiflora, founded by renowned Australian floral designer, Saskia Havekes. "I will always be indebted to the Grandiflora team for the experience and will cherish the memories I have. You couldn't ask for a better opportunity to learn about flowers and putting together compositions, from large-scale installations to the smallest delivery bunch. I developed my creativity and also gained exposure to the day-to-day running of a business." For more than seven years now she has operated solo from her tranquil retreat/design studio, "The Shed". "We have two beautiful swallow birds with peach-coloured chests who nest above us in the roof in summer!" Composting all greenery on site and nurturing good relations with local growers, "who regularly surprise me with something new", the ever enthusiastic and down-to-earth Aleksandra is the ideal partner for any floral project.
www.aleksandra.com.au

RSVP.

Guests: _____

We would be delighted to attend ☐
Unfortunately, we are unable to attend ☐

Please RSVP by 29th April 2011.

To:
133 4
U op Ma

a single flower.
think about you.
forever in my Garden.

Claudia Ghandi

This will be the Winter of our Content...

jonat

133

The Cha
Ceremon
be Indivi
Company

"I often layer scented flowers in my bouquets. Whether daphne and sweet peas in the spring, or gardenias and tuberose in the summer, a waft of something magically fragrant will always be remembered and associated with a special occasion. Arrangements can also be accompanied by bespoke stationery, which I hand-draw myself."

"Kinfolk, *a magazine that brings together an international community of creatives, including artists, writers, designers, photographers and cooks, hosted a Flower Potluck at a quaint little café called* Something For Jess *in Sydney to celebrate the arrival of spring. Guests were asked to bring flowers or greenery, whether from the roadside, corner store, backyard or wild fields, to share with everyone. I brought some of my seasonal favourites: beautifully scented local-grown garden roses, heirloom spider chrysanthemums and sweet jonquils.*"

"WHILE I HAVE AN IDEA IN MIND WHEN WORKING ON SOMETHING, IT'S THE TIME SPENT IN CRAFTING THE FLOWERS, RESPONDING TO HOW THEIR UNIQUE BEAUTY WORKS TOGETHER, THAT ULTIMATELY DEFINES THE END RESULT. FLORAL DESIGNERS NEED TO KNOW WHEN ENOUGH IS ENOUGH. KNOWING WHEN TO STOP CAN BE HARDER THAN KNOWING WHERE TO BEGIN."

"For Nicola and Darren's peach wedding at Lindsay House in Sydney, the bridal bouquet included Australian natives such as coral-pink waratahs, flannel flowers, blushing brides and little puffs of mulla mulla, as well as David Austin roses, peach ranunculus, daisies and dusty miller, wrapped in lengths of velvet and linen ribbon. The tables featured an eclectic selection of jars and vases filled with whimsical spring gestures: cut sprigs, clustered groups and single specimens of poppies, French tulips, irises, wattle, double peach daffodils and cyclamen, to name but a few."

"*At the Sydney launch of the 'Zodiac' fine jewelry collection by Samantha Wills and zodiac illustrations by Kelly Smith, the floral installations were key to decorating the white, empty space of the District 01 gallery. These included a swing used as a base for the SW signature light, with flowers trailing and growing among and around the centrepiece. Balloon vine, asparagus fern, kale roses, begonias, Canterbury bells, posies of lisianthus, phalaenopsis orchids and magnolia branches sculpted the centre of the room.*"

"ABOVE ALL, I LOVE WORKING WITH COLOUR. I THINK COLOUR RESONATES WITH A SENSE OF CELEBRATION. I APPRECIATE THE PURITY OF A SINGLE HUE AND ALSO ENJOY TEXTURIZING COLOURS AGAINST ONE ANOTHER."

"*The arrangement opposite was made for an open day at The Tate @ The Toxteth, organized by the Sydney-based design agency Zed & Bee. Each participating vendor created their own little pop-up to showcase their works and talents. I hung a garden swing in the middle of the space to complement the celebratory atmosphere, using summer blooms such as Coral Charm peonies, garden roses, hydrangeas and phalaenopsis orchids in gelato-y 'ice pop' colours.*"

AMY MERRICK
USA

Not so long ago, one could find a little girl ceremoniously collecting flowers while strolling through the impressive Longwood Gardens in Pennsylvania. "My parents said I couldn't pick any flowers, but I could take ones that were on the ground, so I would fill my pockets with fallen rose petals and rub them on my face." This must be why Amy Merrick today cites the picking of flowers as her favourite part of the design process and why she is so attuned to the power of perfume. "I harbour dreams of being a perfumer and arranging scents in the same way I arrange flowers," she confides. Having initially studied fashion design at university – "I think the attention

paid to colour and proportion in clothing lends itself just as well to flowers" – and having got her first job at a flower shop, Amy realized that flowers had to be a part of her life. "I couldn't imagine going through a winter without them. Life in a big city like New York without a daily natural connection just isn't a possibility. Every week a new flower comes to market. It's a thrill to witness nature progress and to mark time through flowers." Amy has been working professionally and independently since 2009. She has built on her gift for composition and often gravitates towards wild plants – a big bramble of blackberries, for instance – but always imposes a thoughtful restraint and simplicity. Some perceive her arrangements as vintage-looking; all agree they are romantic. Amy also shares her passion by teaching classes at her family's two-hundred-year-old farmhouse. "Seeing students cut from the garden and tackle arranging with a beginner's eye is really rewarding. They have no sense of how things are 'usually' done, so there's a lot of freedom there," Amy muses. "Someone once said that my work made them look at the natural world in a whole new way. They now noticed changes in the flowers and trees they passed on the way to work. Opening up people to the subtleties in the seasons makes me overwhelmingly happy."
www.amymerrick.com

"WORKING AS A PROP STYLIST REALLY HONED MY SENSE OF BALANCE, WHEREAS WORKING AT AN ANTIQUE SHOP HELPED ME AMASS A BIG COLLECTION OF FLOWER BOOKS AND VASES!"

"*I like to walk around a flower market for half an hour or so before I start selecting things. Having a full idea of everything that's available is the only way I can start envisioning an arrangement. I then approach each as its own, trying to focus on colour and movement – the idea of making an arrangement look as though it's been caught up in a light breeze.*"

"I'm not sure I ever perfect a composition; I like to stop a few steps short of 'perfection'. Some of my favourite arrangements are done within fifteen minutes. Sometimes I work and rework things forever, and that's not a good sign. Foremost, I like to arrange flowers so they seem to be growing out of the vase – a natural wildness, but restrained and softened."

ANDREAS VERHEIJEN
THE NETHERLANDS

When Andreas Verheijen accepted an invitation from the Rose Society of Uruguay to give a lecture and demonstrate some of his arrangements, he quickly realized that sourcing flowers was going to be a challenge. He had arrived in Montevideo at the hottest and driest time of the year, local gardens were scorched, and there were no imports to be had. He managed to find an old lady who sold flowers and placed an order for one hundred white trumpet lilies. On the morning of the demonstration, however, to his great dismay, the old lady told him she could not fulfil the order. "When my host asked me if I was alright, I told her that I had no flowers!" recalls Andreas. "She said she would see if some of the attendees could bring white lilies…. When I made my way to the demonstration room, I could see dozens of them. The ladies of the Rose Society had called each other and brought all they could find." Andreas is full of endearing stories, as befits a much in-demand floral artist who has travelled the world and nurtured a passion for nature since childhood. "I used to dig up plants in my parents' garden and move them elsewhere. My parents were not impressed, to say the least, so they gave me a small section of the garden and some pocket money to buy seeds." His village, Zundert, also hosted an annual dahlia festival. "My father was very involved in the building of the flower floats. When I was in my early teens I designed my first, named 'Swan Lake', and contributed many more designs in the years afterwards." No doubt early precursors of Andreas's out-of-the-box creativity. But creativity is not all that is needed for a business to flourish. As Andreas notes, "Working with fresh material is a very specific discipline. You need to be methodical and to have communication skills and organizational, planning and accounting skills. You need to be able to keep cool under pressure." "Flower engineer" *par excellence*, Andreas doubtless has it all. *www.andreasverheijen.com*

"This flower wall was created for Salon/1, a platform for presenting and debating design, which took place in various locations throughout the Amsterdam city centre. My wall was featured in the shop window of the fashion store Kabinet, and was sponsored by the Dutch chrysanthemum hybridizers group."

SALON·1

"This series of 'Engineered Hybrids' was commissioned by the international trend-forecasting magazine Provider, and was intended to inspire designers in general. I chose to dissect plants and reassemble them into new 'hybrids'. Apart from being a proposal towards new varieties, the series was to be seen as a laboratory for shape, colour and texture in a broad sense, rather than just for the flower industry."

"STUDYING AT AN ART ACADEMY AND SUBSEQUENTLY WORKING AS AN
ARTIST HAS HELPED ME LOOK AT DESIGN FROM A WIDE PERSPECTIVE.
I OFTEN COMPARE MY PROFESSION WITH LIFE DRAWING.
ONE FIRST NEEDS TO STUDY ANATOMY AND PROPORTION.
WITHOUT KNOWING THESE, YOU CAN'T SUCCESSFULLY
FREE YOURSELF AND MAKE YOUR OWN INTERPRETATION."

"'Series 7' – portraits of the graduation year of ArtEZ Fashion Design 2013 – was commissioned and art directed by Matthijs Boelee, head of the Arnhem fashion department, and photographed by Louise te Poele. Themes included the individual in relation to excess, colour and texture. Tribal African adornments were among the sources of inspiration."

ANNA DAY & ELLIE JAUNCEY
THE FLOWER APPRECIATION SOCIETY
UK

The Flower Appreciation Society may not be about elitist selection or secretive oaths, but it is quintessentially British. Co-founders Anna Day and Ellie Jauncey conjure up scrumptious arrangements with 'just-picked-from-the-garden' flair. Both have other jobs – Ellie runs a knitwear label and Anna is a midwife – so the company occupies a special place in their hearts. "We met working behind the bar in a pub," the pair exclaim. Anna was in the middle of a floristry course and Ellie had spent summers helping her mother (also a florist) with weddings back home in Wales. A wedding held at the pub was their first joint commission and they quickly realized that they shared a very similar aesthetic. "Then we asked if we could make weekly flowers for the pub, then we bought a camera with the profits, then we thought about getting a website together.

The Flower Appreciation Society was gradual and almost unintentional." The pair now match their informal designs in all shapes and sizes to quaint antique vases and jugs they collect along the way. They try to use English flowers and foliage and to keep their arrangements natural. "The idea of putting diamonds in a rose makes us want to cry!" Operating without a shopfront means that there is no leftover stock. Moreover Ellie and Anna compost their green waste and recycle flower packaging. They wrap wedding buttonholes using old vegetable boxes from a nearby deli and they deliver bouquets in large gherkin jars from the local pub. Also known for their signature flower caps, the pair create work that encapsulates joy and exuberance. "At the Port Eliot Festival, we made flower headdresses all afternoon for the festival-goers. It was lovely to see all these folks adorned with our flowers having such a wonderful time and looking great." The Flower Appreciation Society is somehow evocative of a jolly Victorian age, emancipated for our blissful enjoyment.
www.theflowerappreciationsociety.co.uk

"The ceramic swan vase opposite contains roses, sweet peas, guelder rose and hydrangeas. The flowery pastel crate on this page is filled with French tulips, guelder rose, hydrangeas, dahlias, spray roses and sweet peas."

"OUR DREAM PROJECT WOULD BE TO WORK WITH LOCAL GARDENERS WHO WOULD GROW FLOWERS FOR US. BESIDES, THE BEES WOULD LOVE IT. WE COULD PRODUCE FLOWER APPRECIATION SOCIETY HONEY!"

"A 'not your average florist' headdress can be seen
opposite above, featuring hydrangeas, scabious,
alstroemeria and thistle. The jam-jar wedding flowers
opposite below include garden roses, alchemilla,
mint, peonies and sweet peas. Above is a big shell
vase containing just about everything! It includes
wild sweet peas, scabious, foxgloves, peonies,
delphiniums, hydrangeas, veronica and beech."

"WE TRY TO USE NATIVE FLOWERS AND TO STAY AWAY FROM THE EXOTIC. WE DEFINITELY WANT TO KEEP OUR ARRANGEMENTS AS WILD AND NATURAL AS WE CAN. FOR US IT'S NOT ABOUT BEING NEAT OR USING SYMMETRY."

"Opposite above is a pastel bridesmaid's bouquet, including anemones, sweet peas, narcissi, lilac and ranunculus. A raspberry bridal bouquet is opposite below, with garden roses, astrantia, clematis, sweet peas and peonies. On this page peonies, love-in-a-mist, dahlias and sweet peas fill an old enamel jug."

ARIEL DEARIE
ARIEL DEARIE FLOWERS
USA

When we think of floral works that exude a Dutch still life master's flair, we might well remember the name of Ariel Dearie. This Brooklyn-based designer certainly talks about her craft as a painter might describe their art: "When using a lot of colour, it is crucial to have a good grasp of colour theory." In fact, it is Art Deco and Art Nouveau paintings and tapestries that are Ariel's main source of inspiration; so, too, her highly atmospheric home town. "I grew up in New Orleans – a city so overgrown and lush; our backyard was like a wild jungle. It surely is still one of the most persistent influences on my work to date." Ariel initially studied business. "I'd been planning to open a bakery/café since I was 16. True to my initial ambition, I managed the Five Leaves restaurant in Greenpoint, Brooklyn – an experience that helped me become organized and able to multi-task." Now a full-time floral designer, Ariel creates naturalistic botanical tableaux that deliver timeless charm. Specializing in arrangements with a free-flowing form – "I think allowing flowers air and room to breathe is very important" – she extracts more from less, creating an impression of lavishness while usually employing just three or four well-chosen elements at once. "The seasons are always changing so there are constantly new flowers available to work with," she notes, adding, "I have a strong appreciation for fleeting beauty. It makes it that much more special while it lasts. I love dead flowers and find some flowers to be even more beautiful once they've wilted, or the colour has been drained out." Gazing at Ariel's exquisite compositions, one cannot help but get a sense that they are embodiments of composure and harmony.
www.arieldearieflowers.com

"I TEND TO STICK TO MUTED HUES AND CREAMS,
BLENDED WITH LOTS OF INTERESTING GREEN
FOLIAGE. I ALSO LOVE INCORPORATING NON-
FLORAL ELEMENTS, SUCH AS FRUITS AND
VEGETABLES, EVEN BIRDS AND NESTS!"

"*The arrangement opposite was made for a wedding on the North Fork of Long Island. We used amazing pale yellow peonies, dates and andromeda. For the arrangements above, created for an Indian wedding with a muted palette, we filled antique brass vessels with ranunculus, veronica, freesias and jasmine.*"

"The top left arrangement was made for an Indian wedding. We used lots of warm, bright colours, including these almost fiery peonies and marigolds. For the arrangements top right, we filled a variety of small antique glass vessels with ranunculus, anemones, andromeda and variegated geranium leaves, all in very muted tones. Above left we made an early spring arrangement by pairing garden roses, hellebores, jasmine and andromeda: it's very simple, but it's one of my favourites. The arrangement above right was for a holiday dinner table. We used autumn pear leaves, garden roses, ranunculus, anemones and pomegranates. For the arrangement opposite we used some incredible forsythia that we'd found upstate. The colours on each branch ranged from burgundy to gold to green. We paired this with cream lisianthus and persimmons."

"I ADORE IT WHEN I HAVE THE TIME TO BE LEISURELY AND TO PLAY AROUND WITH NEW FLORAL ELEMENTS. EACH TIME, I SIMPLY TRY TO EMPHASIZE THE MOST BEAUTIFUL TRAITS OF A FLOWER, BE IT THE STEM, COLOUR OR SHAPE."

AZUMA MAKOTO

JAPAN

"WHEN I COMBINE DIFFERENT KINDS OF PLANTS, I TRY TO LISTEN TO EACH VOICE CAREFULLY. I ALWAYS HAVE A STRONG CONVICTION THAT I'M WORKING WITH SACRED OBJECTS AND WITH LIFE ITSELF. FLOWERS ARE ALREADY BEAUTIFUL AND PRECIOUS JUST BY BEING THE WAY THEY ARE IN NATURE. IT'S IMPORTANT TO RESPECT EACH ONE AND TO FEEL ITS DIGNITY."

The cornerstones of Azuma Makoto's philosophy include a devotion to the vitality of flowers, an abandonment to their ephemerality and an absolute comprehension of the way in which they interact with their surroundings. This emeritus artist is a sort of flower whisperer, a botanically tuned seer. His extraordinary body of work is experimental but always respectful. "In order to capture the beauty of plants," he notes, "it's more important to have strong determination than to follow rules. As long as I have this spirit, I truly believe that plants respond to me." Azuma originally studied law at university, but spent all his time playing in a rock band. As he recalls, "I realized that there are many similarities between music and flowers. They are both momentary and inherently unique … and, just as each red rose has a different character, so each sound differs from another depending on the player's state of mind and environment." Azuma's mission is to bring out the latent beauty within each plant through his own hyped-up performance. After fifteen years, his outlook on his work has barely altered, but he has made some changes. He now uses rooted plants alongside cut flowers, and he designs larger-scale projects such as landscapes. "I often use a method that combines the beauty of forms of natural plants and of artifacts, in order to emphasize the beauty of the plants and to transform them into a mass of new life." A firm believer in the benefits of modernity, Azuma remarks, "Technology is really important for my creations for two reasons. First, it's necessary in order to have access to plants that are only supposed to live in a particular place. Second, it can support my ideas when I transform plants into artworks. For instance, if I want to plant moss on concrete, I need special equipment to keep it moist. We have to accept the fact that plants live in modern times, just as we do, so it's pointless to ignore the development of technology when handling them." With a predilection for plants that are "so full of tension that they are about to explode", Azuma makes art that is hypnotizing in all its glorious ambition and confrontation.
www.azumamakoto.com

"'*Shiki 1*' – a pine tree hanging in mid-air inside a metal cube frame – is one of my signature works. *It's the first piece in an experimental series that seeks to propose a new concept of beauty by confining a pine – a symbol of beauty in natural form – to a square frame, representing rules and regulations. Beauty is born out of the friction between nature and artifice. Attention is also drawn to the concept of life and death in a plant.*"

"I USE UNCONVENTIONAL METHODS BECAUSE I'M SEEKING TO BRING OUT THE BEAUTY AND MYSTIQUE OF PLANTS. SOMETIMES I RELY ON A RADICAL METHOD; OTHER TIMES I CHOOSE A SIMPLE ONE."

"The 'Fish Flowers' series seeks to identify a new concept of beauty by combining two aesthetically pleasing life forms – fish and flowers. The flowers are arranged in a water tank filled with swimming fish, so that the fish experience the flowers and the flowers experience the fish. I chose elements of the same colour: two forms of life co-starring in a synthesis of stillness and movement."

"For the 'Bottle Flowers' series I put flowers in bloom, in water, inside bottles. Over time, the decaying flowers and the pigment that oozes out of their petals combine enigmatically, and this creates an indescribably beautiful world. The viewer can see the transformation as the flowers go through their life cycle inside a sealed bottle."

"These 'Collapsible Leaves' pieces show
new forms constructed with leaf work.
Thousands of leaves were folded and
positioned individually. Viewers found
themselves confronted by the fresh vitality
and transformation of this lush foliage,
worked and layered by human hands.
Such is the primitive power that plants
possess, these pieces were elevated to an
almost supernatural form."

"I exhibited this series of works in the Cramped Punk gallery space of the Azuma Makoto Kaju Kenkyusho, or Botanical Research Institute. The ideas that came into my head, inspired by plants, were brought to life on the spur of the moment. The space – dominated by the plants' energy – was rough, and yet delicate at the same time. As part of the process, I destroyed and re-created the pieces."

"By attaching java moss that resembles leaves to a beautifully curved Sabina chinensis dead wood, and then immersing this in water, a new bonsai is created. Bonsai, which usually transform in shape over time, are now transfigured by water and grow even faster. We are able to witness and admire the appearance of a new life form: bonsai in water."

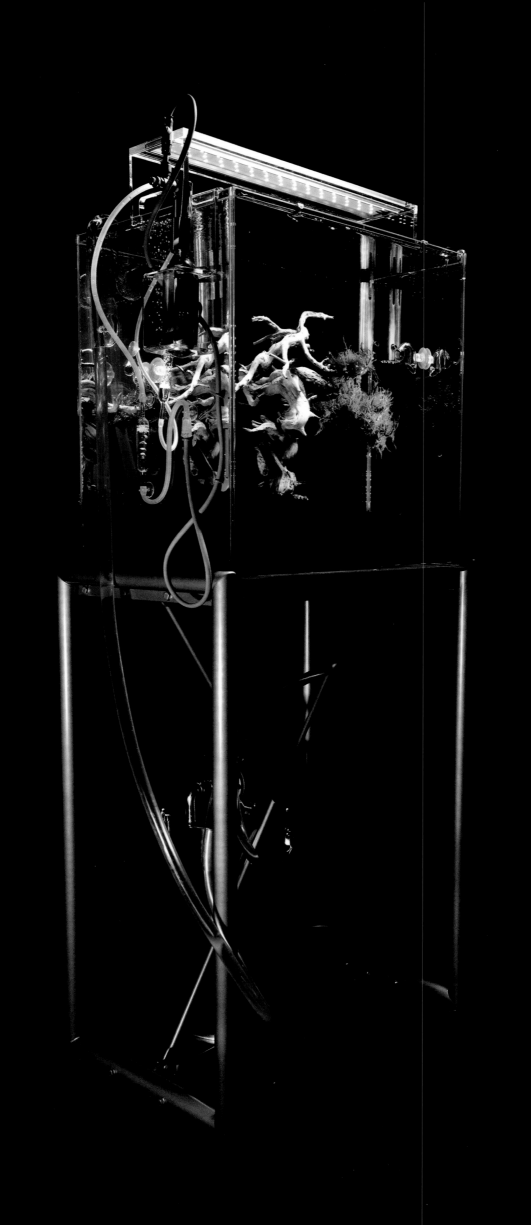

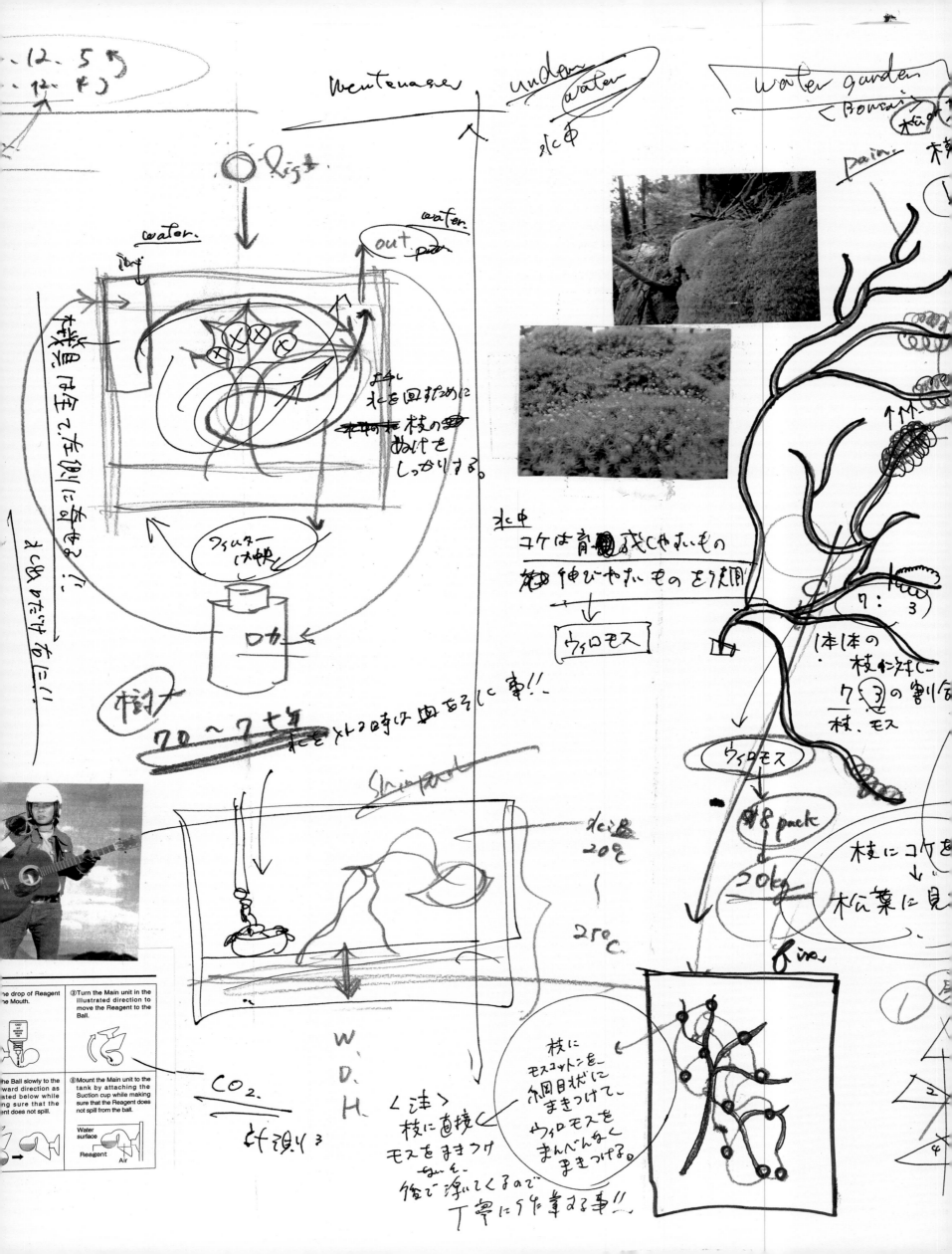

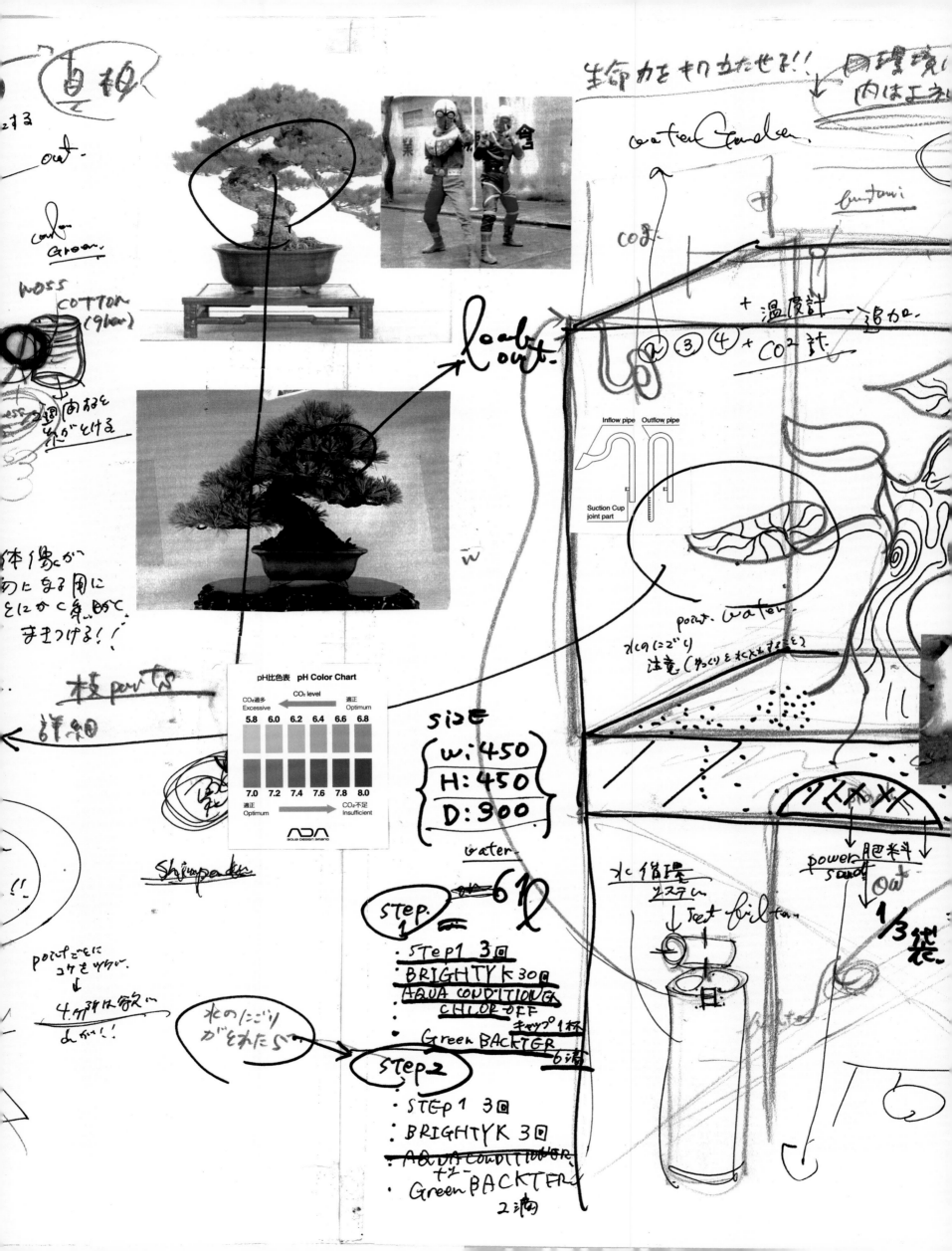

BAPTISTE PITOU
FRANCE

The same maestro who orchestrates some of the most magnificent floral commissions in France – elephants sculpted out of green moss and screens of red poppies for Kenzo's 25th anniversary; thousands of lilies in the Opéra Bastille for thirty years of haute couture by Yves Saint Laurent; and, later, 450 wheatsheaves sewn onto M. Saint Laurent's funeral casket – is swift to declare his fondness for the unassuming little violet. It is this humility that is Baptiste Pitou's great strength. "I am an orphan and was raised by the Apprentis d'Auteuil institution," he explains. "I started working for a florist at fifteen. When I said I wanted to start working, Father Daniel was not too happy, since he'd done everything to make sure I got an education. He was my role model, and I inherited his zeal for poetry, his extreme perfectionism and his creative flair." Baptiste has since forged long-term relationships with many of his illustrious patrons, decorating their homes and styling their events. He oversees all the floral arrangements for the Mandarin Oriental Paris and has his own divine floral corner inside the Hermès shop on the rue de Sèvres in Paris. The apparent simplicity of his arrangements belies their meticulous structure. This high-end artisan compares himself to blotting paper, saturated with intense sensory sensitivity and often teary-eyed. It is easy to understand why when hearing some of his clients' remarks: "At a wedding, someone once said that my display represented a true fairy tale. At a funeral, one guest mused, 'Your flowers are so beautiful, it almost makes it worth dying.' Another client, having just bought one of my rustic bouquets, exclaimed, 'No need to buy a country house!'" Baptiste's own Parisian apartment is always full of flowers, and its inner courtyard is embellished with laurel, rose bushes, jasmine trees, a fountain, mirrors and gravel flooring – a rural sanctuary in the city. Baptiste has the gift of bringing grace to whatever he touches, wherever he is. *www.baptistefleur.com*

"The location was the beautifully restored Château de Vallery, 60 miles south of Paris (previous pages and here). The happy couple were an American and a Frenchwoman, who wanted their wedding to be chic and romantic, like the château. As the village church wasn't available, I suggested we build one of our own, complete with aisle and altar. We made panels of gypsophila and boxes of gypsophila and hydrangeas, using clearly defined shapes to differentiate from the surrounding foliage. The finished installation – which took six people a day, a night and another half-day – was enchanting. The whole atmosphere was wonderful."

"I am responsible for all the floral decorations at the Mandarin Oriental hotel in Paris. Every week we tell our clients a story: that is to say, from the entrance, via the lobby, through to the garden, we use the same variety, like a walk along a country road. For this installation we created 13-foot-high mirrors, pierced with a thousand flowers. Over the weeks the tableaux changed according to the flowers used. Variations included gloriosa lilies (this spread) and orchids (overleaf)."

"I LIKE TO USE JUST ONE VARIETY
OF FLOWER, AND IN PARTICULAR
GYPSOPHILA. WHEN IT'S PRESENTED *EN
MASSE*, THIS FLOWER HAS CHARACTER."

"For this wedding at the Abbaye de Morienval, the couple wanted a rustic 'shabby chic' style of decoration. We placed large arrangements of gypsophila in Medici stone vases at the altar to match the stone of the abbey. For the bouquets we created gypsophila balls suspended on satin ribbons. We also made a bench out of oak branches so that the couple could sit next to each other during the ceremony. The entrance to the abbey was decorated with a large arch of gypsophila. We decorated only a few areas, but they were done lavishly."

"FOR INSTALLATIONS, I WORK CLOSELY WITH MY CLIENTS. NOTHING BEATS THE *COUP DE FEU* WHEN IT'S TIME TO DIVE IN AND MAKE IT ALL HAPPEN: A FIREWORK OF EMOTIONS."

*"For the tables the couple chose huge candelabra, decorated with scented Yves Piaget roses, sweet peas, scabious, mint and Alchemilla mollis. We suspended large, similarly decorated coronas from the ceiling. In the park we hung five hundred white lanterns with **LED** bulbs inside so that the lamps would glow like the moon when night fell."*

"MY ARRANGEMENTS RADIATE SOFTNESS AND POETRY, AND NOTHING IS CONTRIVED. MY STYLE IS SAID TO BE REFINED, ELEGANT AND A BIT WILD."

"A client asked me to remove a pot of crassula that had lost its leaves … and its life! Back in the workshop I saw its wonderful roots so decided to add black/purple Vanda orchids to make an arrangement called 'La baleine et les étoiles' ('The Whale and the Stars'; opposite). For 'Mille reflets' ('A Thousand Reflections'; above left), I used two rings of thorns to bind a bunch of Avalanche roses: I love simplicity and purity, which are always effective. The 'Bouton d'or' ('Gold Button') display above uses proteas and coral-bead nertera: I have long been inspired by the ocean environment, where everything seems mysterious. For 'Plumage argenté' ('Silvery Plumage'; left) I used ornate wiring to tie a bridal bouquet of Vanda orchids, anthurium and anemone seed: I tied them in the shape of a sword so that no one would steal the groom!"

"For 'Le berger et la reine' ('The Shepherd and the Queen'; below left) I wanted to unite the deep colours of **Black Queen** dahlias and fiddlehead ferns, so created a ring of burnt plastic to bring out the tones. The 'Au dessus du lac' ('Above the Lake') display (bottom left) was inspired by my waking from a nap near a lake to see the fiery red sun setting in the grass: I did a sketch in order to reproduce the scene in my workshop, using carnations, iris leaves and a tie of senecio. The tulips in the 'Heureux épicurien' ('Happy Epicurean') arrangement below stand upright in a cup of water, while hydrangeas are trimmed with scissors to form a sort of vase around this."

"For the fantasy landscape in 'Fugitif oriental' ('Oriental Fugitive'; opposite above), butterflies from the famous taxidermy store, Deyrolle, flutter past a tree made of white callas. For 'Fusion impériale' ('Imperial Fusion'; opposite below), soft tee grass, like a cloud of water, and rustling carnation leaves give the impression that the bouquet is about to evaporate."

"*Hand-tied arrangements are typical of my designs – open, colourful and airy. Each flower has space and freedom and looks as if it's flying. With this kind of depth and the different levels, you can always see something new, no matter what angle you're looking from. Most of the flowers here are summer seasonals, available from local markets.*"

BJÖRN KRONER
GERMANY

Near Bleiswijk in the Netherlands is a greenhouse used by the Anthura company to grow rare anthurium and phalaenopsis that are usually reserved for research and breeding. "I was lucky enough to get access to these exclusive flowers during the Interflora World Championships in Shanghai," recalls Björn Kroner. This prize-winning Master of Floral Design graduated from Grünberg under Peter Assmann at the age of 23 – the youngest possible age – following an apprenticeship in floral design and work in a flower shop. He spent the next two years in the US, Japan and Spain, working in creative development, product presentation and teaching. "That opened up an entire new world to me," he says. Now known for displays showcasing a wide range of hues within a particular colour group, and mixing a variety of flowers in the process, Björn recalls, "A good friend in the international art world once told me that what I do is 'applied art'. I agree." Björn also tries to follow the advice of his mentor, Monika Knoop-Tausch: "Everything has to flow like a stream." "I make sure I combine flowers and colours so that tension arises, yet the ensemble remains harmonious." Björn and Monika also organize creative sessions, such as Jackson Pollock-style action painting or pottery-making. Björn relishes the unexpected ideas prompted by group work, and "what I have learned I happily pass down to the next person". Having received acclaim for his installation at the 2012 Festival of Flowers in London, this regular contributor to *Fusion Flowers* magazine recently toured Korea and Australia. His next major project is "der grüne Tisch" (the Green Table) – a multidisciplinary space for hire: "You'll be able to organize pop-up dinners at the table, for instance, or it can be turned into a catwalk. Everything imaginable will be possible." Björn's vision is a move away from garden-variety practices towards a sublime level of lifestyle at the intersection of Art and Entertainment. *www.bjoernkroner.de*

"THE IDEA IS TO CREATE A DESIGN THAT DOESN'T
GIVE AWAY EVERYTHING AT FIRST SIGHT, BUT
WHERE YOU DISCOVER NEW FLOWERS AND
TEXTURES EVERY TIME YOU LOOK AT IT."

"This location in Recklinghausen and the people who were present are very special to me. We made a wreath out of hand-cut sheets of transparent paper normally used by architects. I coloured each sheet a different shade to form a colour wheel. The circles were then affixed to an acrylic ring, which stood on acrylic feet to raise the wreath. I selected mainly seasonal flowers to suit each shade. I like the texture of the paper with its rough-cut edges, and I like the colours. It's a very light and summery arrangement."

"I wanted to shoot this arrangement against the background of colour drips from some action painting seminars. The vases were produced by Fürstenberg, a high-end porcelain manufacturer. I was involved in the design – mainly the lids, which can be used to help build floral constructions. Samples had just arrived and I thought it would be interesting to play with colours and flowers and to create a grouped arrangement with vases that are normally used individually. The flowers include Rosa omeiensis, Odessa calla lilies, opium poppies, peony hybrids, mophead hydrangeas, red hot poker hybrids, Cotinus coggygria and plumed cockscomb."

"I love to combine my skills and come up with something new and different that can't be bought off the shelf. I made this impromptu container as a table decoration for a barbecue dinner by manipulating chicken wire, covering it with papier mâché, then colouring it layer by layer from light to dark. The idea was to have an organic vessel in a natural environment, with a summery floral feeling. I filled the container with summer roses, blue passion flowers, Allium giganteum, Caucasian scabious, Gerbera jamesonii *'Tattoo',* Cosmos bipinnatus *and hydrangea hybrids."*

"I NOW HAVE THE LUXURY OF BEING ABLE TO USE ALL SORTS OF FLOWERS AND MATERIALS FOR MY WORK, BUT REGARDLESS OF WHETHER I USE EXTRAORDINARY PLANTS OR MORE COMMON ONES, I LOVE TO 'IMPRESS WITH LESS'. IN THE END THIS IS WHAT MAKES GOOD FLORAL WORK."

"This table setting was impromptu. I found the painted wine bottles in a corner; the pink plastic cups I'd got in Italy. Most of the flowers are summer plants. I like to buy them from local growers. It's also nice to use flowers that are in season. The scene was set for a beautiful evening, sharing my passion in life with friends."

CARIS HAUGHAN & VANESSA PARTRIDGE
PRUNELLA
AUSTRALIA

ntering Prunella on the quiet main street of Kyneton is like stepping into a cabinet of floral wonders. This enchanting botanical folly is filled with dazzling arrays of blossom, glass domes, prints and other curiosities. It is the gateway to the baroque imagination of its two proprietresses, Caris Haughan and Vanessa Partridge, who both moved to the Victoria countryside at the same time, neither with any formal training in floristry. "We met, and our shared passion became larger than the two of us. Prunella was born." Vanessa's background in marketing, PR and media helped create the brand identity, while Caris's experience in hospitality management guarantees that client expectations are fulfilled. Of Prunella's signature style, one thing is clear: the pair do not hold back. "We love using big things to create theatricality – huge sculptural branches, roses on long, sweeping, spiky stems, multiheaded hydrangea clusters, dramatic foliage, grapevines, artichokes, green tomatoes, recycled farm machinery… We've also been commissioned to improvise with what we find in a client's own garden. Bringing the outside – with all its wildness – in, is our drive." The pair daydream of a no-budget commission, "creating the arrangements for a film like Sofia Coppola's *Marie Antoinette*". One sensational real-life project involved four marquees at the Melbourne Cup – "a challenge creatively, logistically and collaboratively. We had to dream up, plan and install creations in differently themed sections of the racecourse under extreme time pressure, just the two of us. And we pulled it off!" Prunella promises to become the ultimate destination for all things "floral pleasure"-related: workshops, pop-up shops, even a garden design service. This pair are not resting on their laurels.
www.prunella.com.au

"We use a lot of cut glass for our arrangements because we love the way it reflects light. In this case, we were also inspired by Caravaggio, who always had something dead or decaying in his paintings, hence our dying yellow leaf. This arrangement was also all about movement, with the curves of the tulips and the Queen Anne's lace reaching up above."

81

"These flowers were for a country wedding at a family home in the Pyrenees in Victoria. Peppercorn trees can be found everywhere up there, so the delicate weeping foliage and berries became a feature in our arrangements. The bride also wanted lots of colour and we were only too happy to oblige. The height of summer meant dahlias, roses and billy buttons."

"For this dinner in an old red-brick industrial substation, our client wanted a pop of colour and something bold, and we wanted to bring some fresh green to soften the space. Together we decided on an installation of hanging trees. The pop of colour came in the use of neon pink rope, which we zigzagged across the tree tops like a web."

"WE HAVE AN ORGANIC
APPROACH TO FLORAL
DESIGN AND WE EMBRACE
SCALE TO CREATE ORIGINAL,
ARRESTING ARRANGEMENTS.
WE FOLLOW INTUITIVE RULES
ABOUT SHAPE, COLOUR
AND BALANCE, AND –
EVEN THOUGH THERE IS
METICULOUS PREPARATION
BEFOREHAND – WE ALWAYS
FREE-FLOW ONCE WE
START CREATING OUR
INSTALLATIONS."

"*These arrangements were made for a beautiful wedding in Daylesford. The bride's favourite colour was green, and she loved foliage and texture (our kind of bride!). We used seasonal foliage gathered from the area, and added texture with local hydrangeas that were just starting to turn those fantastic antique colours. We also sourced locally grown Italian rose hips, and added some cream- and buff-coloured garden roses just to set the whole thing off.*"

CLARISSE BÉRAUD
ATELIER VERTUMNE
FRANCE

"FLOWERS AND PLANTS HAVE THE ABILITY TO SWAY ALL OUR SENSES, AND THAT'S PRECISELY WHY I'M CONSTANTLY SO PASSIONATE ABOUT THEM. I LOVE THE EXCITEMENT OF BEING ABLE TO ASSEMBLE RAPIDLY, TO FINE-TUNE QUICKLY, TO ENHANCE POWERFULLY."

Have you ever thought a floral arrangement looked so perfect, so natural, that it actually seemed to be growing out of its vessel? This is the impression that Clarisse Béraud attempts to convey with each of her compositions. Needless to say, she is as much poet as she is artisan: "I have an extraordinary colour chart before me… In my hands lie floral shapes, corolla, fruits, leaves, seeds, sepals… Every new morning brings a new floral wonder… Happiness is endlessly reinvented." Clarisse's maternal grandfather ran a nursery, and she remembers deciding that she would make a living working with flowers after helping friends of her parents to sow some sweet peas when she was just twelve. More than a decade ago – after studying with her mentor, Alain Cianfarani, for five years – Clarisse set up her own practice in Paris. Atelier Vertumne now caters to both private and corporate clients at the higher end of the market. Concocting spectacular bespoke compositions for demanding aesthetes, Clarisse recalls: "There was one particularly challenging commission from a Swiss couple – an Arabian Nights extravaganza to be set up in just three weeks, with all of Switzerland's restrictions on flower imports." At the same time, Clarisse is aware that the art of flower arranging should be shared and is a great opportunity for social bonding, so she has launched two-hour-long affordable weekly workshops where individuals, private parties and businesses can create their own bouquets using farm-fresh flowers under the supervision of the Atelier's staff. This attests to her pragmatic qualities and explains her uncanny ability to construct the most exuberant displays without sacrificing accessibility. She refers to hydrangeas as her "staple", as much for their texture as for their colour-ways, but she also has a predilection for fragrant plants such as clematis, honeysuckle and soapwort, as well as rustic varieties including meadow anemone, lady's mantle and grasses. Clarisse's signature style reveals the most beautiful aspects of flora in the most lyrical and harmonious way possible.
www.atelier-vertumne.fr

"This was a table installation for a project about a cinema-themed wedding. Working with scenographer Jean-Luc Blais, we featured glass-bauble-shaped vessels – which we often use to enhance a poetic mood – together with pink-champagne-coloured asparagus fern and floral arrangements based around hydrangeas, white dogwood, rowan, garden roses and moss."

"For the Lenôtre Indian Summer party at Le Pré Catelan restaurant in Paris, Jean-Luc Blais and I brought to life 'the art of receiving' based around the theme of 'squarely square'. Our entire composition was made from dahlias."

Michelle

INDIAN SUMMER

"IT IS ESSENTIAL THAT MY WORK IS EASY TO
APPRECIATE, THAT IT CREATES AN IMMEDIATE
EMOTIONAL CONNECTION ... AND OF COURSE IT
MUST BE FULL OF CHARM. THE UNPREDICTABILITY
OF FLOWERS IS AN ASSET: THEY CONTINUALLY
SURPRISE, ENCHANT AND DELIGHT ME."

*"These compositions were created for a
press presentation of spring/summer 2013
trends. Jean-Luc Blais and I created an
'imaginary dinner' with a boudoir-like
ambience. The suspended arrangements
were of jasmine and anemone. The other
arrangements were made with jasmine,
spiraea, hydrangeas, anemones, peach tree
branches and garden roses."*

DAN TAKEDA
DAN TAKEDA FLOWER & DESIGN
SINGAPORE

"I HAVE NO INTEREST IN EMULATING WHAT OTHER FLORAL ARTISTS ARE DOING; BECOMING A PUPIL TO OTHERS IS NOT WHAT I WANT. WHAT I'VE ALWAYS WORKED FOR IS TO HAVE A DESIGN STYLE LIKE NO OTHER; A STYLE THAT CAN BE TRACED ONLY TO MYSELF."

A square carpet of lush green moss with a single fuchsia moth orchid flower-head resting on one corner, like a brooch pinned to a cushion, exudes potent simplicity. "Less is more" in the most manifest way: Dan Takeda is Japanese, after all, and ikebana philosophy permeates his methodology. But he can also revel in "more is better", as seen in one tableau teeming with flowers in every shade of pink. Whatever the composition, serenity ultimately prevails. Dan's style involves taming his plants via a mesmerizing, somehow illusory interpretation. "I feel so grateful towards Nature that I want my work to impress; to exceed expectations," he admits. He always knew that floral artistry was his vocation, but he first graduated from the Department of Industrial Engineering and Management at Kanagawa University. At the age of 24, while working part-time at a popular flower shop in Tokyo, he finally mastered his technique and began to make a name for himself. A move to Singapore in 2008, where he now lives and works, was the incentive to launch his own business, Dan Takeda Flower & Design. The elegance and quality of his sleek bouquets instantly appealed to luxury corporate customers, including Chanel, Louis Vuitton and Gucci, who entrust him with decorating their boutiques throughout the city, and also private clients via his online shop. Dan's style is permeated with youthfulness: classic with a hip-hop twist (Nujabes-style, as per his favourite musician). He delights in bringing his independent vision and national aesthetic to an eager audience. "I was recently invited to perform a demonstration, in full Japanese gear, to an audience of five hundred. It was a first for me, and really daunting, but I'm glad I was able to make a positive impression on so many people at the same time. In fact, making people happy is crucial to me. One day I'd like to go to an orphanage in Myanmar and teach kids about flowers." For now, Dan is concentrating on a new phase: flowers for weddings. "Hopefully, this will help polish my style even further, all the while establishing my position as a recognized flower artist."
www.dantakeda.com

"I got the inspiration for this arrangement from the Garden of Temples in Kyoto, Japan. The historic temples are tastefully laid out, with a unique beauty. When I tried to make an arrangement with flowers, I came up with this piece, which includes snake grass, lisianthus, fresh moss, anthurium, hydrangea, cymbidium orchid, chrysanthemum, amaranthus, guo shan mao, camellia leaves, teasels and honesty."

"*With this arrangement I wanted to make the most of the individuality of each bloom and to make the viewer look at the flowers with new eyes. Inspired by modern art, I came up with the idea of making the flowers look like a piece of art. Included are eremurus, delphiniums and viburnum.*"

"This composition was inspired by painting. In challenging myself to make an arrangement that looked like a painting, I used lilies, roses, peonies, spray roses and calla lilies."

"The theme of this piece was playfulness. Insectivorous plants and flowers never usually intersect. Putting them together makes a piece of art. I wanted to see people's surprised faces when they saw the insect-eating plant nipping the flower. Featured are an African violet and Venus flytraps."

DOCTOR LISA COOPER
AUSTRALIA

Inspirational figures for Lisa Cooper include the artists Marina Abramovic, Bill Viola, Francis Bacon, Joseph Beuys and Albrecht Dürer, architect Adolf Loos, florist Constance Spry, the "little flower" Saint Thérèse of Lisieux, the philosopher Simone Weil and renaissance man Antonin Artaud. "My work with flowers is a part of my art practice as a whole," explains Lisa. "My only ambition has been to make art. There was some early confusion as to medium – I have at times in my life been obsessed with both dance and theatre – but I was once described as 'looking like' I was born to work with flowers, and that made sense." For Lisa, flowers coincide with metaphysical references and religious archetypes, and this is rooted in her early years. "My most powerful memory of flowers is when my father died, when I was thirteen, and how strongly they analogized his life and death." Identifying her father's passing with the inherent transience of flowers may have shaped Lisa's soulful attempts at recapturing something of that defining moment, each work bearing the hallmarks of an homage to him. She also notes: "My aesthetic flair is reminiscent of both Catholicism – as in decadent, gold, complicated; beauty as transcendental – and Protestantism – austere, elemental, clear; beauty as bound to the earth." Her favourite stage in the process is making. "There is an intoxicating energy in the 'work', in placing elements and responding to an ever-changing composition until there is a moment of peace and finality." Cultural high-brows, mavericks and arts aficionados are among Lisa's fans, and her work has been commissioned by many respected institutions, including the Museum of Contemporary Art Australia, the Sydney Theatre Company and the Australian Ballet. "Many of the people I work with show me a space, then I come back to them with a concept, and then their trust and knowledge of my work allow me to create in situ. However," she adds, "there is a chasm between an idea and its execution, as there are so many variables, particularly when you're working with living elements." Doctor Lisa Cooper works with them all beautifully.
www.doctorcooper.com.au

"I'm attached to garden roses in a hue that's like
a 'British red'. I'm also fascinated by iconography
and see bundles of the roses as being held by saints.
I can't get enough of them and use them often, as the
red seems to 'punctuate' other tones."

"I was commissioned by stylist Jolyon Mason to create some 'blue beards' for Manuscript magazine. I began by imagining all the options. 'What could count as blue? Should the beards be a composition of mixed elements or one type of flower? Should they be constructed on a framework?' In the end they were painstakingly adhered to each model, bloom by bloom."

"*Deutsche Bank Sydney approached me about a work for a dinner to celebrate an Anish Kapoor exhibition. On a site visit, I proposed 'mirroring' a beautiful Kapoor Sky Mirror piece with an equally imposing flower 'dish'. We then built and suspended a ten-foot structure and I used many different types of fern as the base. I punctuated this with elements such as carnations, orchids, rosemary and mint. The palette was restricted to green, yellow and lemon, to both mimic and contradict the marble interior.*"

"IN FLOWER COMPOSITIONS, AS IN ALL ART
COMPOSITIONS, THE CONCERNS ARE LINE,
FORM, TEXTURE, COLOUR AND BALANCE."

"Tiffany & Co. commissioned me to create pieces for the launch of their Bondi Junction store on 13 February 2013. Working within the constraints of the store and its limited surfaces, I used a metal 'plinth' structure that I had designed and made, and filled its vessel to capacity with undulating branches of five types of gum. For an expression of romantic love I filled four Bohemia crystal vases with fragrant garden roses grown locally. I knew that the punch of ruby red would sing against the backdrop of Tiffany blue, and that the height and scale of the arrangements would elevate the status of the 'common' eucalyptus."

EMILY THOMPSON
EMILY THOMPSON FLOWERS
USA

It feels as if a young Bacchus with grapes in his hair might make an entrance at any minute. The setting is so plentiful and fruitful, and suffused with baroque beauty and a veiled menace. Emily Thompson's virtuosity extends even to her surroundings. She lives in a neo-Romanesque mansion – "a sort of ruin, in a tiny apartment with a little windowsill garden; I don't do flowers at home" – but she surely doesn't hold back elsewhere. "I want to make wild and weed-y work that feels alive and maybe a little dangerous," she confides. Her compositions elevate the spaces in which they are placed and complement everything around them. Monumental in essence, even when small in stature, her arrangements are notably sculptural. "I worked briefly at a flower shop in college, and after that I worked for artists and taught sculpture. It all contributes to my way of thinking and making," notes Emily. "My floral company was launched in 2006, and I've been able to make sculptures out of the delicate and infinitely varied materials that are flowers ever since." Emily's strongest botanical memories and associations are of the wild outdoors, the lichen carpets and maple alley near the house where she was born. Her vision is naturally tinged with a woodland mood – the antithesis of floral foam and aluminium wires. For one spectacular event she used beetles and moths, and she has a reliable roster of foragers who supply her with her favourite wild plants. *Vogue* named her "the Florist in New York", and she was even invited to design the White House Christmas. "We planted gardens inside the ballroom. The effect was somewhat austere but altogether dramatic and wild." Emily's dream destinations for her floral arrangements include the Coliseum, the Parthenon, the Blue Mosque, an ice hotel, the Great Pyramid of Giza and the Taj Mahal ("not the one in Atlantic City," she quips). On being asked what her next ambition is, she does not surprise with her answer: "I am building a temple of beauty." Aphrodite may soon join Bacchus. *www.emilythompsonflowers.com*

"Our former studio and shop in Brooklyn, where favourite brass and cast-iron vessels hold summer-foraged grasses and branches. This display was a study in green, using all-local wild material to express the season. We must have just emerged from a cold spring, evidenced by the snowshoes tucked in the corner. The flower guillotine hangs above these delicate materials."

"This arrangement was made for a private event at a client's home. It was a study in shapes – a crescent moon, sitting atop a vase. I love to pull a cantilever to a nearly absurd proportion. I also love these materials: their strong, distinctive petal forms, the contrast, and the combination of exotic with mundane. I've been playing with lilies, trying to see them in new ways. Fruit is also always exciting to use, as the flower's metaphoric future. I used quince on the branch, bee balm, Asiatic lilies, a little Solomon's seal, hosta foliage and wild clematis. Everything was locally grown except for the clematis, which came from California."

*"Here I was adjusting a centrepiece for a summer
gala – an Italian picnic at Lincoln Center to
honour the fashion designer Valentino Garavani.
Baskets held abundant, explosive and highly edible
arrangements. The design indulged my love of quince,
oak and other strong, graphic branches. They were
meant to bring the fruity linens to vivid life."*

"FOR ANY COMMISSION, I LIKE TO FIND OUT
AS MUCH AS I CAN ABOUT THE CONTEXT
FOR THE PROJECT: THE CLIENT, THE HISTORY
AND THE ARCHITECTURE. FROM THERE, I TRY
TO BE AS FREE AS POSSIBLE TO ALLOW NEW
POSSIBILITIES TO ENTER."

"Opposite are photographs showing the construction of a large wedding arch that was used in a photo shoot. It was made with wild blackberries and rambling roses, which we got in six-foot lengths, mingled with more conventional roses. The location was a beautiful Catholic church that boasts the oldest stained glass in the US. The second photo shows the arch amid the effects of a smoke machine brought in by the photographers, which soon after set off the fire alarms!"

"Above is a wedding altarpiece from a different event. The arrangement is full of cybister amaryllis 'Tarantula', my favourite."

"A GOOD FRIEND DESCRIBED MY WORK AS 'GRAND AND SCULPTURAL, OFTEN FOREGROUNDING WILD, FORAGED MATERIALS IN MAGNIFICENT STYLE'."

"Peony season lasts for just a month in our garden, so I take extra care to savour each bloom as it comes out of the field. The gorgeous variety seen here was new to us and happened to bloom just as the first wild roses were opening and the last of the ranunculus were in flower. Combined with brodiaea, grasses and wild rose foliage, the bouquet captured the fleeting moment when so many treasured elements were peaking during the same window of time."

ERIN BENZAKEIN
& FAMILY
FLORET
USA

We may have found what seems like the Garden of Eden somewhere in Washington's Skagit Valley. Endless varieties of organic flowers flourish on two acres of field rows and in ten greenhouses. Welcome to Floret Flowers, an oasis you may not wish to leave. The day that Erin Benzakein sold her first blooms – a bundle of sweet peas that prompted the recipient to re-live old memories – she went home and started implementing immediate changes. "I tore out the veggie garden and re-planted it all in flowers." Once the seed of Floret was planted, abundance and prosperity were inevitable. Now both advocates of local consumption and floral art lovers from all over the globe have lauded Erin and her family. "I'm addicted to research," notes the constant gardener. "I do variety trials for fun. My bravura has kept me going through rocky patches, slow starts and scary times, while my research bug has led me to work with an amazing range of flowers and foliage in a short span of time." Erin embodies the literal meaning of "down to earth", revelling in getting her hands dirty in order to uncover rich bounties. She also epitomizes a new breed of entrepreneur, pioneering a floriculture that relies on sustainable practices. "I would love to see wholesalers and designers connecting more with local growers and sourcing fresh produce instead of flying it in from halfway around the world." On strolling through her flowers, Erin quickly becomes excited to start on new arrangements. "Big pieces, such as urns and large vases, go quite fast. I love dramatic wild statement pieces, and I think my excitement speeds things up," she says. "Centrepieces or low arrangements often take a bit of time, since securing all the elements in a 'pin frog' can be a little tricky." In line with her sensual spirit, Erin also has an unusual predilection: "I love weaving edibles – cherry tomatoes, strawberries, baby apples, raspberries, bush beans, herbs, carrots – into bouquets, as well as airy elements so that the slightest breeze can catch a component." To get started, this ambitious achiever's advice is simple: "Just skip your latte once a week and buy a posy of sweet peas instead!"
www.floretflowers.com

"IN ONE YEAR I GREW FORTY-
SIX VARIETIES OF SWEET
PEAS, THIRTY-FIVE VARIETIES
OF ORNAMENTAL PEPPERS
AND SIXTY-FIVE VARIETIES
OF CELOSIA, JUST SO I
COULD EXPERIENCE EVERY
POSSIBLE FLOWER I COULD
GET MY HANDS ON."

122

"The span between late fall and true winter can often feel eternal. Not quite time to rest but too dark and cold to be really productive, it's an awkward period for creativity and focus. It was during one of those dark days that I created this bouquet. Using the last of the rose hips from the garden, along with privet berries, parsley foliage, cardoon leaves and akebia vine, I chose to thread in lots of billowy peach and coral roses from a local grower to create this moody, romantic arrangement."

GIOTA GIALLELI
ANTONELLO
GREECE

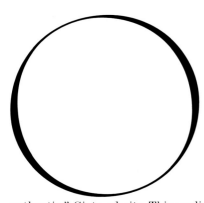verlooking the National Garden in Athens, Giota Gialleli's house offers spectacular views from every window and every door. Nature literally flows in and embraces the many books and pieces of antique furniture in the building. "I enjoy a luxury environment and anything that is real and authentic," Giota admits. This applies also to Nature. "My first memory of flowers is of a giant rose bush with hundreds of red blooms beside an eighty-year-old vine with a very thick stem. I remember the sunrays passing through a hundred shades of green – absolute happiness." Imprinted by this early sensory overload, it is as if Giota has been aspiring to achieve the same emotional pull in her work ever since, from the simplest bouquet for a passing customer to the most prestigious commission for the Athens Concert Hall, the prime minister's mansion or a celebrity client's home. Giota also takes care to change the hotly anticipated window displays of her shop, Antonello, regularly. "A lady saw my shop window one night and called me the next morning to say that it had helped her get through a difficult day." Inspiration can strike from anywhere, though a subtle evocation of Greek tragedy never goes amiss: "Tempests, the sun, the moon, love, hate and human passion…" Giota also draws on her own character traits – stamina, stubbornness, curiosity, a dose of vanity – to aid her in her accomplishments. What impresses the most is her awe-inspiring sense of spatial awareness, combined with her immaculate design flair. These can be seen to particular advan-

"IN THE MORE THAN FIFTEEN YEARS THAT I'VE BEEN WORKING AS A FLORAL ARTIST, MY APPROACH HAS BECOME BOLDER AND I'VE ACQUIRED ENOUGH SELF-CONFIDENCE THAT I CAN TACKLE MORE DIFFICULT PROJECTS HEAD-ON. MY CONCEPTS CAN STEM FROM A SCENT, A PASSING IMAGE, A COLOUR, A SUNRAY."

tage when she decides to display her precisely crafted floral sculptures against a background of historic sites, street fountains or beaches, where, against all odds, the compositions seem entirely at home. "Floral art is at an elementary level," Giota declares. "There is a long future ahead. I strongly believe that one day it will take its place among the other arts, because I suspect it might well turn out to be even more vital than music."
www.antonelloflowers.tumblr.com

"For this 'Pink in Paradise' arrangement, I used layers of pink delphinium, limonium 'Emile' and sweet pepper. The inspiration was a ballet performance by my daughter on the theme of spring."

"*My inspiration for 'The Nest' was an intriguing nest I found on a walk in the woods. I used artichoke leaves, muscari, pink roses, almond blossom, limes, senecio and dill.*"

"I FEEL THE NEED TO EXPERIMENT WITH THE IMPACT THAT
FLOWERS HAVE ON HUMAN PSYCHOLOGY. AS A RESULT
I TRY TO SUMMON UP STRONG EMOTIONS THROUGH MY
COMPOSITIONS. I WANT TO MAKE EACH RECIPIENT AN
INTEGRAL PART OF MY ARRANGEMENTS. I BELIEVE THAT
MY WORKS HAVE AN AURA. EMOTION DOMINATES, AND TO
THAT EXTENT SIGHT IS PRACTICALLY UNNECESSARY."

"For a friend's birthday party in the Mount Lycabettus neighbourhood of Athens, I worked with a plethora of plants, including daisies, eucalyptus, Cotinus coggygria 'Royal Purple'*, viburnum, antirrhinum, spiraea, Casa Blanca lilies, sunflowers, freesias, fig branches, aspidistra, tillandsia, Grand Prix roses and Colombe de la Paix calla lilies."*

"THERE ARE TIMES WHEN I HAVE TO BE FLEXIBLE BECAUSE OF A LACK OF MATERIALS. OTHER TIMES I JUST LET GO AND SEE WHERE AVAILABLE MATERIALS LEAD ME. THESE KINDS OF DETOURS ARE USUALLY MORE CREATIVE."

HARIJANTO SETIAWAN BOENGA

SINGAPORE

"I SEE MY WORK AS AVANT-GARDE IN A THEATRICAL WAY, YET SURPRISINGLY I ALSO LOVE MINIMALISM. MY HOME REFLECTS THAT: JUST A FEW SIMPLE POTTED PLANTS AND NO FLOWERS. AT HOME I LONG FOR EMPTINESS AND SERENITY IN ORDER TO LET MY MIND REST AND TO GET FURTHER INSPIRATION. IT'S ALL ABOUT MY IMAGINATION AT PLAY, NOT ABOUT VISUAL STIMULI."

Harijanto Setiawan's father offered some sage advice when his son told him he wanted to become a floral artist: "Be a tiger in a small cage rather than an ant in a huge tree." Harijanto obeyed, and is now one of Singapore's most revered practitioners. He originally trained and worked in architecture, "but after about eight years, first in Jakarta, then in Singapore, I decided it was time to breathe some freshness into the floristry scene, using the knowledge I had gained in architecture as my inspiration". Boenga – derived from *bu-nga*, Indonesian for "flower" – was born in 2002, and success followed when a major Singaporean bank ordered custom-made Christmas trees for each of its thirty branches. Harijanto rapidly became the go-to floral wizard for the region's rich and famous, though he notes: "My creative style is now more flamboyant, dramatic and expressionist." Whether preparing a lavish wedding for an Indian mogul, or thousands of custom-made elements for an artistic installation, or a "flower kingdom under the sea", Harijanto infuses all of his works with a spirit of otherworldly fantasy. This is always, however, anchored in thorough preparation. "No matter how big or small the project, free-flow will only occur once a solid basis has been set," he asserts. For his efforts he has been garlanded with numerous accolades – "Best Florist" by Singapore *Tatler*; a Silver Leaf Award at "International Floral Art 10/11" in Belgium; third place at "Fusion Flowers International Designer of the Year"; Gold and Best of Show at the Singapore Garden Festival; "Designer of the Year" at the prestigious President's Design Award. Harijanto's arrangements are noted for their plays on shades of green, possibly an homage to the Indonesian rainforests of his childhood. His favourite flowers include the bold and beautiful gloriosa lily. "A flower is like a candy in a jar," he says. "If you eat it you will enjoy the sweetness, and if you leave it there it will still be beautiful inside the jar. That's why I believe in the healing and benevolent power of flowers; a sort of 'Flower Peace'. The day may come when flowers unite all the humans in the world and prompt us to become a more peaceful humankind."

www.boenga.net

"This 'Shower of Blessings in Paradise' piece was exhibited at the Putrajaya Flower Show in Malaysia. It features Vanda and Mokara orchids, gloriosa, craspedia, orchid root and iris leaf. I also used fishing line in two tones – transparent and luminous green."

"This head adornment – called 'The Queen' – was made and photographed at the Blue Mansion in Penang. The theme was ancient beauty in the Chinese era. I used red garden roses, hypericum berries and red dahlias."

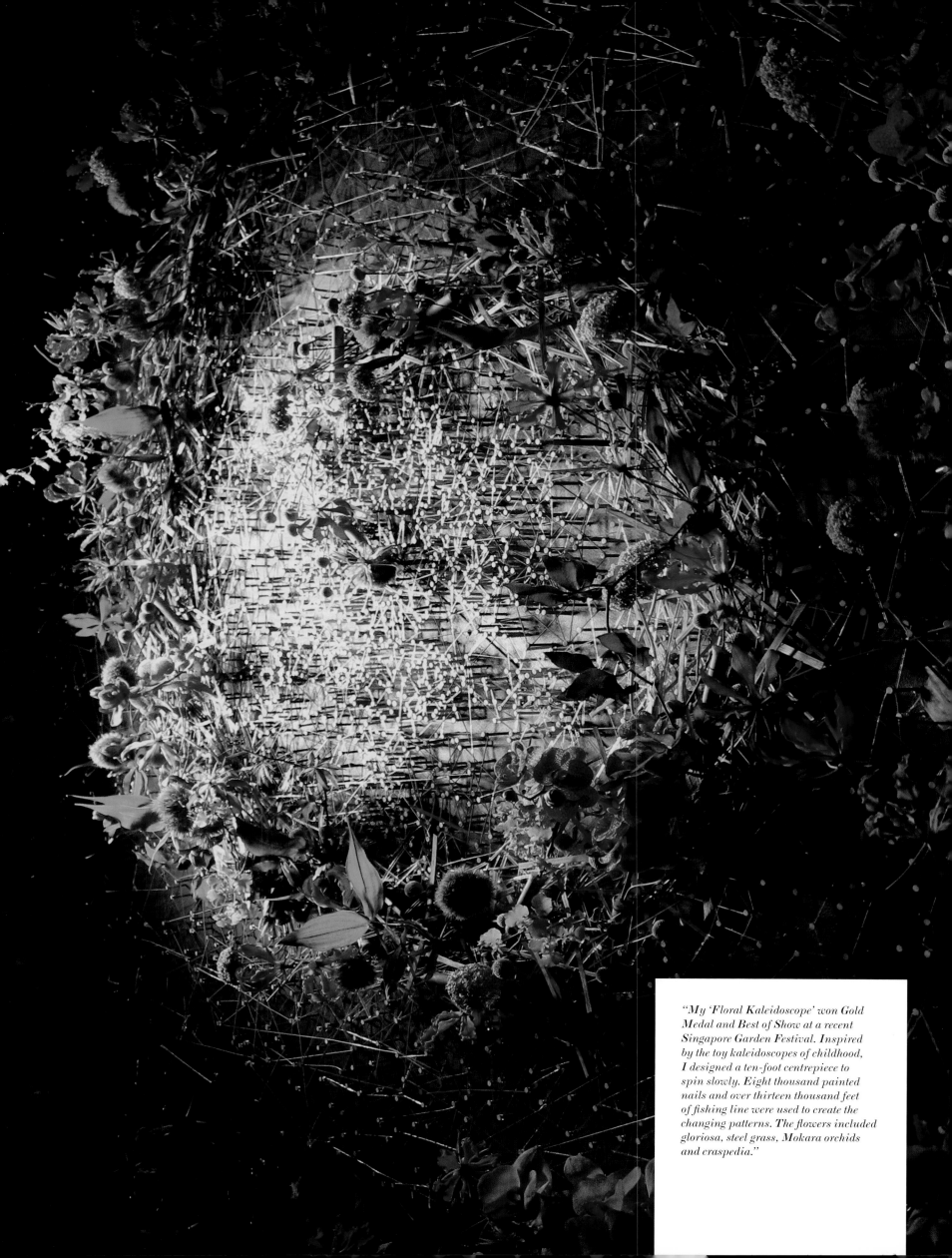

"My 'Floral Kaleidoscope' won Gold Medal and Best of Show at a recent Singapore Garden Festival. Inspired by the toy kaleidoscopes of childhood, I designed a ten-foot centrepiece to spin slowly. Eight thousand painted nails and over thirteen thousand feet of fishing line were used to create the changing patterns. The flowers included gloriosa, steel grass, Mokara orchids and craspedia."

"This piece – 'Noodle!' – was made by using finely sliced calla lilies to create the noodle effect. The bowl was constructed out of dried lichen."

"I used steel grass to create the cup for this piece, known as 'Movement'. It was awarded Gold by Fusion Flowers magazine, who named me 'International Designer of the Year'."

"I was asked to create an arrangement for the new European Central Bank in Frankfurt. This impressive building has two towers, connected by an empty space. I created a basic geometric design from gum wood, which appears to float in the air, and filled this with an opulent, baroque-like arrangement using Fritillaria imperialis, Dianthus caryophyllus *and tulip hybrids. In this way, I connected old and new."*

HEIKO BLEUEL
GERMANY

In the case of ordinary floral compositions, flowers are often arranged to look pretty, end of story. The work of Heiko Bleuel could not be more different. "I aim to surprise; to encourage the idea that we can interpret familiar things in unfamiliar ways." In order to do this, Heiko concentrates on his containers as much as his flowers. "I challenge myself to combine durable elements with non-durable. If you can convey an impression of eternal life with flowers sitting in beautiful receptacles, then the lifeless receptacles themselves should also be able to appear more 'lively'." Heiko therefore works almost exclusively with hand-crafted containers that can tell a story. "In an age when most things are industrially manufactured, it's important for me to convey my appreciation of traditional craftsmanship to my customers." He has many years of experience to share. "By the time I was eight, it was clear to my family that I would become a gardener. But, years later, once I'd become professional, I realized the job wasn't living up to my idealized expectations. Then when I was nineteen – and already training to be a florist – I went to a national flower competition. When I saw all the creative artworks being made by florists, I knew I was on the right path." Heiko qualified as a "Floristmeister" in 1996 and went on to work in Luxembourg, Belgium, Switzerland and Italy. After a stint at the German publishing house Profil Floral, he went freelance. "I had more time to produce permanent floral objects, which was the start of collaborations with Bulthaup Studio and B&B Italia. My work began to move more and more into the field of interior design." Heiko has also forayed into product design: his "Light Colours" lamp for Anthologie Quartett even made it onto the cover of *AD* magazine. In 2006, he opened his own shop in Frankfurt. "Along with flowers and plants, I sell unique objects such as premium terracotta by Francesco del Re, Murano glass by Arcade and Bohemian glass by Anna Torfs. I also run a programme of exhibitions for young designers. My customers are design-oriented and are always trying to find ways to improve their interiors. Good florists have a unique opportunity to give their clients floral pieces that are the icing on the cake."
www.heikobleuel.de

"IMAGINING SOMETHING – PICTURING IT IN YOUR MIND – CAN BE VERY EXCITING. I OFTEN SEE THINGS SO CLEARLY THAT I THEN DON'T FIND IT NECESSARY TO ACTUALLY REALIZE THEM ARTISTICALLY. BUT ONCE I'VE ABSORBED THE THEORY, WHAT IS IMPORTANT IS THE IDEA. IF YOU HAVE AN IDEA, THE FLORAL WORK WILL FEEL LIKE A STROLL…"

"The idea for this arrangement came from architecture. The pot, covered with stuck-on beech leaves, reflects the ground-plan of an upside-down Egyptian pyramid. I cut off the tip to give the container a better balance. Spring flowers grow from the surface area of the pyramid."

"The art of Old Masters such as Jan Brueghel the Elder, Jan Davidsz. de Heem and Jacob van Walscapelle was the inspiration for transporting still lifes to modern times. The snail, for example, indicates a slower life; the dove, death. Also included are wild strawberries, blackberry brambles, showy lady's slipper and common beech."

"Floral still lifes from the Renaissance to the Baroque have always inspired me. The idea of many different flower forms, often from very different seasons, gathered together in a single floral work, is fascinating. During my training, we were asked to re-think and re-interpret the old scholars. I made a highly controversial tied arrangement that used about sixty different flower shapes and styles and no in-filling foliage. Nearly twenty years later this type of floral grouping is all the rage!"

HELENA LUNARDELLI ATELIER HELENA LUNARDELLI

BRAZIL

There is no doubt – seeing the saturated colours and sheer luxuriance of foliage mixed with tropical flowers – that we are in the presence of an exotic ambassador. All the alluring, lush, carnival glamour spells one word: Brazil. São Paulo-based Helena Lunardelli was 27 and working in fashion when two friends who owned a flower design studio invited her to become a partner. "It was when I grabbed a pair of shears for the first time to prepare my first arrangement that I felt this exhilarating sensation: I understood the reason why I had been born! I began going to the market and learning more about the trade." Pushing the theatrics, Helena's compositions are often elaborate, with an air of fabulousness. She is an ardent fan of the Companhia de Entrepostos e Armazéns Gerais de São Paulo, the largest flower market in Latin America, and has even written a delightful guide singing its praises and advising on how to purchase flowers there. A journalist once credited Helena's own work for preserving tropical species native to Brazil, and specifically for including local flowers in both classical and contemporary arrangements ("she said this reminded her of the work of landscape architect Roberto Burle Marx"). Helena adds, "I was extremely flattered because, until then, I'd never realized how much of my work was based on the use of tropical flowers and on valuing our local culture and flora." What's more, the pro-

"MY WORK IS KNOWN FOR ITS USE OF UNCONVENTIONAL ELEMENTS: BARRELS, SINKS, PAINT CANS ARE TURNED INTO VESSELS, AND I ALSO SOMETIMES STYLE WITH FEATHERS AND TOYS. BUT I BELIEVE MY STYLE IS CONTEMPORARY, COMBINING THE OLD AND THE NEW AND AVOIDING THE OBVIOUS."

fusion of her arrangements extends to a broader generosity. Helena established the Flor Gentil (loosely translated as "Kind Flower") project in 2010. Reliant on volunteers, this upcycling project is based around re-using floral arrangements from weddings and parties. "We collect flowers after events and create new arrangements, personally delivering them to homes for the elderly. We also train low-income workers and donate flowers to decorate events being held by low-income community members." How refreshing to encounter such a talent, her craftsmanship entrenched in her native culture and her creativity perfectly attuned to altruism.

www.atelierhelenalunardelli.com.br
www.florgentil.com.br

"*I made these flower arrangements for the very special wedding of a bride who had originally split up from the groom, was due to marry another man, then bumped into her old flame and decided to stay with him forever. She loved orchids and hydrangeas as well as sober colours such as burnt orange and antique rose. My inspiration came from the idea of a happy, light, autumn wedding. I used a lot of foliage – tangerine, mandarin – as well as lilies and snapdragons. For the ceremony I chose narcissus, which reminded me of the myth and which I hoped would protect the couple: the idea of seeing each other like a reflection.*"

HOLLY VESECKY &
REBECCA UCHTMAN
HOLLYFLORA
USA

ailed by some as the best floral duo in Los Angeles, Hollyflora have quite a reputation to maintain. "You see the stuff that comes out of Hollyflora? The girls just get it," is a typical comment, this time from the owner of an art gallery the day "the girls" were setting up an event there. But Holly Vesecky and Rebecca Uchtman prefer to keep a low profile – testimony to their devotion to their craft. They tackle the creation of a rustic bouquet with the same verve as they embark on a fantastical sculptural project. "We are innovators (artists) within a specific spectrum between media and tradition (artisans). Our style can be described as 'wild and earthy Californian, with a dusting of Old World'," says Holly. Rebecca adds, "I'm probably most charmed by the occasional dark element. Something macabre – sharks' teeth, tiny rodents, bird skulls, antlers – always makes the flowers seem prettier." Holly's gift may be traced back to when she was a line cook and ice cream scooper, "sculpting with food", while Rebecca, as a hairdresser, learned theories behind colour, shape and balance. The pair's widely varied works tend to make a lasting impression. "Together with friends and volunteers we built a floral volcano. This ten-foot-tall replica of Mount St Helens had a subwoofer inside that rumbled until three cannons erupted in petals," Holly recalls. Of their "Eagle Nebula" piece, she says, "I collaborated with electrical engineers, who came up with a non-sequenced lighting scheme that made the flowers flicker very subtly, like the night sky inside a geodesic dome." These oscillations between performance and design keep Hollyflora's creative momentum rolling and the orders flowing. The pair's success can also be attributed to down-to-earth operations. "We have an organic, biodynamic orchard that we cut from in Ojai. We'd like to develop a small retreat there. Guests would be able to cut from the gardens and pick the fruit from the trees. A gardener's Eden … with lots of booze," the duo laugh. Their plan for Hollyflora's Bacchanals is sure to succeed.
www.hollyflora.com

151

"In the organic orchard at Mulberry Haven in Ojai, 170 fruit trees grow on two acres, including mulberry, Sunshine grapefruit, carob, pomegranate, blood orange, plum, sapote, persimmon, Anna apple, fig, jujube, peach, macadamia, loquat, lemon, lime and Catalina cherry. Flowers are picked from the floral cutting gardens."

"We find so much inspiration from the redwood groves in Big Sur. Filtered sunlight on the forest floor meets chaparral in this bouquet: poppies and ranunculus with fun, textural brunia. For the bouquet opposite we felt inspired by the abundance of our orchard in spring. We cut ivory runner roses and mulberry leaves from the property and added local camellia and ranunculus blossoms for an unstructured 'master gardener' feel."

"NO TWO SPECIMENS ARE THE SAME, AND,
WHILE THERE ARE CONSTANTS IN SEASONS,
EACH NEW FLOWER HAS ITS OWN UNIQUE
PERSONALITY, JUST LIKE PEOPLE."

ISABEL MARÍAS
ELISABETH BLUMEN

SPAIN

"I HAVE THE FEELING FLOWERS KNOW WHERE THEY WANT TO BE, AND I JUST LISTEN TO THEIR DEMANDS! I SCOUT ANTIQUE SHOPS AND FLEA MARKETS TO FIND SPECIFIC VESSELS FOR ARRANGEMENTS, AND THEN I JUST PUT ONE FLOWER NEXT TO THE OTHER – AS A POET WOULD ARRANGE WORDS – TO CREATE THE MOST EXPRESSIVE AND BEAUTIFUL COMBINATIONS."

Some flower arrangements have the power to transport us to a beautiful parallel world: a world of exquisitely evocative colour, crystal vases, and tea canisters resting on floral-patterned tablecloths. In this instance, behind the intricate, delicate prettiness, we might also detect the faint melody of a flamenco lament. Isabel Marías Luca de Tena founded her flower arrangement and event company, Elisabeth Blumen, in 2010 in Madrid. It has since established itself as a purveyor of arrangements with instant classic power, now on offer in Isabel's recently opened first shop at Number 75 Calle Mayor. She in fact originally studied fashion design and always thought she would devote herself to the industry, "but I came to feel very disillusioned and lost. Quite out of the blue, flowers became first a hobby, then a passion, and finally my business," she recalls. "I started out by helping a florist who arranged all the flowers for a big company once a week. That special day became my favourite time of the week, and I would return home with leftover flowers in a bag, anxious to make my own arrangements. I soon realized that I wanted to be surrounded by flowers all the time." The first time Isabel went to a wholesale warehouse she felt she had arrived in paradise. "All those plants were within my reach, including my favourites such as astilbe, white anemones with black stamens, fragrant garden roses, berries of all kinds and autumn leaves." Still today, when she opens the delivery boxes she receives from Holland, she exults: "It feels like tearing the wrapping paper off to discover your most anticipated gift at Christmas." The broader the choice of flowers, the better. "I like to think my work is thoughtful and careful. Although I never plan a composition very much beforehand, I certainly have lots of references in my head." Isabel follows her intuition, and it works. "Some people have told me they didn't pay much attention to flowers until they saw my arrangements, and that really touches me." She adds, "Working with flowers puts me into a 'meditative' state that I find almost mystic and transcendent." Avoiding repeating herself has become an obsession that allows her to feel present and excited about pushing her craft. It is this perfectionism that means her art never fails to enchant and seduce.

www.elisabethblumen.com

"I'm passionate about colours and their infinite amalgamations, and I love creating ephemeral beauty. The small bouquet in the vintage porcelain teapot (above) is made using garden roses, tulips, hyacinths, Geraldton wax, veronica, wallflowers and eucalyptus. The arrangement in the metallic tin (left) is made with dried and preserved flowers such as hydrangea, lavender, papaver, achillea and broom."

"The arrangement in the glass bottle was made with Romantic Antike roses, astilbe and pittosporum. The little wedding bouquet was created using a mix of fresh and dried flowers, including astilbe, craspedia, yarrow, matricaria and mini-chrysanthemums, tied with vintage lace."

"The wedding wreath on this page is made with preserved flowers such as rose, chrysanthemum, lavender and matricaria. The wild wedding bouquet (opposite) includes flowers such as snapdragon, astilbe, matricaria, Queen Anne's lace, asclepia, tea roses and viburnum, tied with bobbin lace."

JOAN XAPELLI
FLOWERS BY BORNAY
SPAIN

T he team behind Flowers by Bornay is to floral art what Ferran Adrià is to contemporary cuisine: revolutionary. But for founder Joan Xapelli Bornay (to give him his full name) success was far from assured. An insecure, introverted teenager, his imagination was fuelled by a fantasy world. "Comic books, Marvel heroes, and the epic movies of George Lucas and Steven Spielberg offered me an escape route," he recalls. Although fascinated by creative artists and designers, he never thought he could pursue an artistic career himself and consequently "vegetated" through various mundane jobs until he became an administrative clerk for the Catalan flower trade. Transformation was at hand. Joan ended up trading flowers throughout the whole of Spain. After thirteen years, he realized he could put his insider knowledge together with his vivid imagination and create a unique model for floral art. "I was

the happiest person on earth when I realized I could combine flowers and my fantasy world and make a living out of it!" Now he and his teammates, Fàtima Valldeperas and Marta Vidal, have built a "think-out-of-the-box" forum for their ideas. Steering clear of preconceptions and expectations – whether concerning "floral ethics", the use of traditional components or the need for a background in floral art as a prerequisite for working with them – the company functions more like an experimental lab than a flower studio. By implementing their creative vision with determination and rigour, the team have fashioned a distinctive Bornay vocabulary. But, as Joan notes, "We are neither activists nor corporatists; we just follow our own path." Notwithstanding the company's leader-of-the-pack reputation, the team organizes regular, sought-after workshops, where "we share our secrets with people from all over the world". Using extraordinary materials and techniques, they improvise compositions that are as exhilarating as they are ravishing. Like a movie director, Joan has found a way to tell exceptional stories.
flowersbybornay.blogspot.com

"Opposite I can be seen practising one of my signature techniques, spray painting. On this page the 'Tailor's bouquet' is inspired by old-fashioned tailoring. The carnations and white peonies, evoking femininity and elegance, are tied with bright ribbons and a tape measure."

163

"WHEN WE WORK, WE FOLLOW THE
'BORNAY RULES'. FOR EXAMPLE, TO OBTAIN
OUR SIGNATURE LOOK WE BAN THE
USAGE OF FOLIAGE FILLERS AND WE USE
UNCONVENTIONAL TECHNIQUES TO HELP PROP
OUR ARRANGEMENTS TOGETHER."

"The centrepiece opposite is titled 'Henri Matisse' and consists of painted succulent plants. The centrepiece below is called 'Night Lights' and was made using hydrangeas and painted echinops. Both are in line with our vision: presenting flowers in new, innovative ways that are modern and carry endless possibilities."

"Our 'Pixel' concept was born out of the wish to replace the colourful sand that is often used for the base of compositions. We brainstormed and came up with the idea of using coloured foam blocks. These 'Pixel Mirror' centrepieces were inspired by video games of the 1980s and are composed of hydrangeas, sedum, celosia, zinnias, peonies, roses and brunia. We cut each 'pixel' to size from large foam sheets, which we painted individually."

"EACH ELEMENT OF A COMPOSITION HAS TO
HAVE A MEANING AND PLACE, YET THEY ARE
ALL 'COLLAGED' TOGETHER AS A HARMONIOUS
WHOLE. FLOWERS HELP ME TELL STORIES
IN A VISUAL, BEAUTIFUL WAY."

"We came up with our 'Carpet' concept soon after the company was founded. We had been commissioned to decorate the local W Hotel and spent days thinking about the project. We wanted something inspired by the sea floor, and that is how we decided to create aquatic worlds of our own ... in flowerpots. This opened up infinite possibilities for a 'Carpet' series. The centrepiece shown here is called 'Mars' – after the planet that inspired it – and is composed of carnations, craspedia and some rocks!"

KALLY ELLIS
MCQUEENS
UK

I t takes great courage to steer one's life in a brand new direction … especially if the change is based on sheer hunch. But that is exactly what Kally Ellis did over twenty years ago, when she decided – quite literally – to follow a dream, which then turned out to be her dream. "I dreamt that I was a florist, and it was a vision so strong that within six months I had opened my business," she recalls. "To this day I still apply what I learned then: don't over-think things, and don't over-research. Ignorance is bliss. Trust that your passion and determination will see you through." Kally's first shop was in Shoreditch, London, on the spot where the aunt of the fashion designer Alexander McQueen used to run a florist boutique. Now Kally has a flagship store on Old Street and an outlet inside Claridge's hotel, and she and her team are on the speed-dials of some extremely prestigious clients, including the Connaught and Berkeley hotels, the luxury brands LVMH, Tom Ford and Mulberry, and *Vanity Fair* magazine for its annual post-Oscars party ("being flown around the world is definitely a 'pinch myself' moment"). At the core of McQueens' creative manifesto is an avowal for crisp simplicity and stylish understatement. Minimal flowers, repetition of vases and use of local varieties are signature traits. Kally always employs her gifts – whether for hand-tied bouquets or large-scale event planning – to great effect. "Quite often it's about thinking outside the box and being clever with mechanics – for example, using transparent fishing line to make flowers look as if they're floating." Kally is also quick to credit her co-workers: "My brilliant team are hardworking, loyal, talented and inspirational. Many come from art or design school, so they're not governed by the traditional rules of floristry. I place greater emphasis on creativity." One of the highlights of Kally's career was the twentieth anniversary of McQueens, "seeing my wonderful staff and clients together – some of whom have been with me from the beginning – all gathered in one room, celebrating everything we've achieved". Just like one of her heroines, *Pride and Prejudice*'s Elizabeth Bennet, who Kally hails for "carrying the flag for strong, independent women who know their own mind", Kally has life-enhancing qualities; and hers have also served to make our world a more glamorous place.
www.mcqueens.co.uk

"This landscape of fishbowl-shaped vases showcases a signature McQueens look: green hydrangeas, alliums, purple clematis, white eryngium, pink gypsophila and Alchemilla mollis."

"White arums and Selaginella plants adorn a wooden block. To me this represents Zen. It's tranquil, and effortless, and for the moment."

"FOR ME IT'S ABOUT DESIGN DISPLAYS. ONE TYPE OF FLOWER: THAT'S OUR SIGNATURE LOOK. I'VE ALWAYS LIKED CLEAN AND TIDY DESIGN."

*"This is a contemporary classic **McQueens** look: a trio landscape that combines drama and romance. The flowers that feature are some of my all-time favourites: La Belle pink roses, pink hydrangeas and Sarah Bernhardt peonies."*

"We created a beautiful display for the Mulberry spring/summer 2012 fashion show at Claridge's hotel. It was mystical and magical. I structured trees with clouds of English flowers, including roses, hydrangeas and gypsophila – typical English blooms – in mint green and peach, adorned with ivory. To complete the look, Mulberry had giant English garden gnomes made!"

KRISTEN CAISSIE
MOON CANYON DESIGN
USA

"I LET MY FLOWERS SPEAK FOR THEMSELVES, AND THEREBY FOR ME. I TEND NOT TO OVER-WORK A COMPOSITION, SO AS TO KEEP IT NATURAL. I ALSO INCLUDE A LOT OF WILD VINES, FERNS AND WOODLAND GREENS TO ANCHOR MY ARRANGEMENTS. PEOPLE GENERALLY RESPOND BY SAYING THEY LOOK EFFORTLESS."

In most of Kristen Caissie's works, a salvo of ravishing flower-heads, both large and small, punctuates a mass of intricate foliage. This is a celebration of "Love is in the Air"-style romance, with maximum impact. Three key factors under-pin the look: first, Kristen used to lie as a child under her grandmother's blossoming lilac tree and "become drunk on its scent, like a little bee"; second, she studied Romantic lit-erature, specifically poetry; and, third, her work with flowers simply feels like second nature. "While I was on an academic track, I stopped to smell the roses and never looked back," she quips. "But before I could fully commit to floral design, I tried my hand at window display and prop styling. I really enjoyed using all sorts of materials to create fun and interesting décors. Then I moved to Los Angeles, leaving behind a happy home in Boston and my great display business. But something called me out West. When I arrived, I had no plan to speak of. I was at the beginning again; free to make a new start." Moon Canyon Design was born, and Kristen teamed up with her friend Amy Lipnis to position the new business as an authentic artisan venture. Each bouquet, wreath and installation is handcrafted and each is infused with poignancy: blooms overhang freely, and ensembles are loose, evoking the delectable abandonment we feel when we're in love. At the core of Kristen's character is "her unwav-ering desire to do what makes me happy", and this outstrips any worries and in turn transmits itself to the customer. "Some blooms last longer than others," Kristen notes, "but each is beautiful and able to shine in the moment given. Who am I to deny myself beauty, whether it's for a long or a short moment! Perhaps we all have something to learn from living in the moment it takes to enjoy the life span of a daffodil."
www.mooncanyondesign.com

"This shoot was done in the spring at a dear friend's studio space. I love her wide open, white loft. I think the flowers look so pretty in all that white light."

"What I adore about this arrangement is the way it feels as if it was found on the forest floor in springtime. For me, its subtle colour and foliage conjure up feelings of romance. I find it beautiful how it stretches and reaches so freely for what is beyond its vessel. Included are fritillaria, a garden rose, poppies, umbrella fern, spiraea and lilac."

"*This arrangement was an afterthought – made,
essentially, from leftovers. I almost never use such
bright colours, so when I made this I was pleasantly
surprised. I love how full and wild it is. Playful,
colourful, bright: so not my usual! Included are
viburnum, poppies and foraged foliage.*"

"*I wanted to create a bouquet that was an atypical bridal look. The result (below), made with branches and pods, is woodsy yet romantic, and I adore the contrast of the burgundy and green. Opposite left is fritillaria, so sensitive yet majestic: I was going to put this into an arrangement, but realized it needed to be alone, as it holds all the beauty in its own movement and shape. The fern and spring blooms opposite right fit very well on this vintage chair. Wreaths and crescents are so beautiful and can accent almost anything. Opposite below is a wreath made for the textile designer Rachel Craven. Her clean style inspired me to make something that would resonate femininity and beauty, while not feeling too 'flowery'. Again, I took the chance to make flowers in the round.*"

LINDSEY BROWN
LINDSEY MYRA &
THE LITTLE FLOWER FARM
AUSTRALIA

"I DON'T BELIEVE IN TRYING TO MAKE FLOWERS INTO SOMETHING THEY'RE NOT. ANGLES AND STRAIGHT LINES ARE NOT REALLY MY THING. FOR ME, IT'S ABOUT TRYING TO CAPTURE A BIT OF THE OUTSIDE AND BRING IT INSIDE. I AIM FOR MY COMPOSITIONS TO HAVE DEPTH (OF COLOUR, TEXTURE AND FORM), EMPATHY (SYMPATHY WITH THEIR SURROUNDINGS) AND MOVEMENT."

Lindsey Brown is crystal clear on what nurtures her soul. "Colour excites me. Texture fascinates me. Nature feeds me." This artist/artisan – a self-described chameleon – in fact started out as a weaver. Today she says, "I still think of myself as a weaver who just got distracted! But in many ways floristry is a form of weaving." Two main experiences shaped her path towards serious, full-time floristry. "Working part-time for seven years for an established florist's boutique in Melbourne, and working for my good friend Melanie Stapleton, owner of Cecilia Fox, were essential in my development as a florist and as a person." Lindsey also credits a certain optimism, a good dose of hope and a touch of pig-headed determination as vital traits that have led her to where she is today. Pragmatism has also helped. "What do plants teach us, if not that beauty fades but will come again? I believe my role as a human being is to be as happy, healthy and honest as I can be. I do this by creating and sharing beautiful things. The world will always need more beauty." The Little Flower Farm reflects Lindsey's commitment. "The farm aims to educate both the public and the industry about how to live with nature in a more harmonious way. It's organic and runs on permaculture principles. I focus on growing heirloom varieties, promoting biological diversity and breaking down the concept that flowers are a distant, mysterious luxury." When it comes to arranging, the excitement of potential combinations is what exhilarates Lindsey, and these days that part of the process involves her walking outside in the fresh air and looking at the world around her. "I feel that this slows me down and makes me see details that one often misses, and it makes me appreciate those little moments." A neighbour recently returned a vase to Lindsey with a note attached, explaining, "It's bad luck to return a vase empty." The neighbour, who had previously told Lindsey she knew very little about gardening, had gathered up some aromatic purple basil gone to seed and some pink nerines that had popped up in her yard, and had put them in the vase. "It was one of the nicest gifts I have ever received," says Lindsey. "What I loved was that she had gone outside and picked what was available to her. I thought to myself: 'Now this is what I'm talking about!'"
www.lindseymyra.com

"This large bouquet was commissioned for a small winter wedding. Despite – or maybe because of – the grey skies at that time of year, I wanted to create something light and summery to match the youthful, carefree nature of the bride. As it was fallow season on the farm, the flower choices were dictated by my ethical commitments as regards buying in product. The poppies, stock, carnations, roses and silver suede were purchased from local growers; the remainder was respectfully foraged from gardens – mine and friends' – and roadsides. The ruby stems of the foraged bramble rose, the vibrance of the succulent flowers and the pinkish tones of the abelia calyx are what unify and ground the many ingredients. They provide depth and cohesion, while the native foliages lend form with their natural drape and arch. These elements give the bouquet its loose, wild feel."

186

"*On this day, I was channelling my inner Dutch Master. It was early winter, the skies were grey and the flowers were moody. The arrangement had been ordered for a dinner party, and I wanted it to have that intimate but dramatic Renaissance feel. Inspiration came from the autumnal hawthorn branches, which I had been watching turn and catch the light for weeks; just a few tenacious bushes still held leaves. The golden crab apple was also essential for the overall effect. I was so excited to find a foraging site for these expressive little fruits. The grass and seeded gum were also roadside finds, while the tulips, jonquils and roses were chosen from local growers to match the evocative textures. When it came to colour combinations, the pinkish-toned roses were the only thing I could get at the time that had that 'antique', burnished tinge. In the end, the contrast lent itself well to the theatrical ambience of the evening.*"

"The footed centrepiece is not widely seen in Australia, but I adore the nostalgic abundance of this style. I used a metal flower stay, or 'frog' (the type often seen in ikebana work), to secure the short stems in place – a technique that's necessary with such a shallow vessel. The palette was influenced by the trend for peach and coral blooms – a colour range I personally adore. However, since the arrangement was being made in the depths of winter, with the farm lying fallow, my flower choices were dependent on what I could find locally grown by small conscientious growers (the interesting thing about fashions in floristry is that, as much as a designer might want to create a certain look, if the raw product isn't being grown then you just can't have it!). So the jonquils, poppies, carnations and roses were bought in, and the rest I foraged and gathered. As always, it was the found elements that excited me most – the jasmine vine and the grass, so fine but with such a magical blend of tones. The joy is in the details."

LOTTE LAWSON
LOTTE & BLOOM
UK

"The colours and softness of spring flowers are a sight for sore eyes after a long winter. Here I stripped back almost all of the branches to the tips to make tendrils, and worked with the natural curves of each branch to create a frame supporting the main body of the arrangement. I used forsythia, flowering currant, hellebore, hyacinth, rose and ranunculus."

W hen Lotte Lawson was around 20 years old, she watched a television programme profiling different vocations. The segment that stood out for her was the one about the day in the life of a florist. "I remember thinking I really wanted to do that, although it took me a few years to actually get around to it." Once she did, Lotte surpassed everyone's expectations, including her own. "In our first year, we made the Top 5 in *The Independent* newspaper's '50 Best Florists'." She goes on to admit, "I seem to have an almost obsessive interest in horticulture. It's just something I find endlessly fascinating. I notice the details with a keenness I don't have for anything else." Through her business, Lotte & Bloom, she is able to express her infatuation freely. "Her creative style is a lot like the Mitford sisters'," a friend once observed. "Quintessentially British, but not afraid to go out on a limb." Lotte says of herself, "I'm quite mercurial, so I get tired of things quickly. Working with flowers feels dynamic, and to be able to move fast is greatly appealing. What's more, you don't have to live with your mistakes for too long, as they die!" She loves to work on commissions for private clients, as she feels that entering and dressing someone else's home is a privilege. "The best arrangements usually happen when you're working instinctively," she says. "There are some very loose rules on proportions I adhere to, but then again I probably break them all a hundred times over in practice. I think it's vital to 'play' with flowers; to work with them as if nobody is watching. It's a chance to immerse yourself in the creativity of the whole process." But running a business is not all about creativity. "A career in flowers is so intense," Lotte points out. "It's physically and mentally demanding, and you need to have nerves of steel. The days start early and are long, long, long. But flowers get under your skin and once you've fallen, you fall hard. There's really no hope for you after that!"
www.lotteandbloom.co.uk
thefloralcoalition.blogspot.com

"*The brief for these bridal flowers was to create
something soft and gentle that would work beautifully
with a delicate beaded dress. I chose small dahlias
so as not to overpower the other elements. I also used
asclepia, which is always a bit of a race against time:
I love the look of it in bud, but when it blows out it
looks fluffy. I think it worked nicely here. The other
elements were zinnias, spray roses and oak.*"

"*For these table arrangements I used rudbeckia, nutans, brassica, celosia, delphiniums, amaranthus, cordyline, hydrangeas and marigolds. I loved mixing up the tropical nutans with the more traditionally 'country' flowers. It shouldn't work at all, but it does. The colours were almost neon; the black cordyline probably has a lot to do with that.*"

LUCIA MILAN
BRAZIL

T he floral gene was rather slow to evolve in the case of Lucia Milan and her mother, celebrated São Paulo florist Aparecida Helena Leme. "My mother always had flowers at home," recalls Lucia, "and we used to go together to the flower markets, where we would get lost because I couldn't help becoming distracted." But, despite constant exposure to her mother's world, Lucia did not want to go into floral design. That changed when, years later, Aparecida Helena casually asked Lucia, who had become a fashion stylist, to help her with some sunflower arrangements. "I had recently married, and the long and hectic hours attached to fashion were becoming difficult to manage," Lucia remembers. "Helping my mother was an epiphany. I suggested we launch a business together, and I've never looked back." Lucia launched her solo career – "a major transition" – once she felt it was time to channel her own creativity. "I really enjoy doing the arrangements myself: choosing the right vase, defining the mood, handling the flowers. My signature touches include arrangements that bend to one side and arrangements with a different back and front." She adds, "Give me twenty silver glasses to decorate bistro tables and I will do each of them differently." Lucia's hands-on approach serves a romantic, shabby chic yet naturalistic style that follows no trends and draws on sustainable practices. Despite being much in demand for celebrity weddings and luxurious parties, Lucia describes herself as "a hippie at heart". "My home is my sanctuary and where my office is. The surroundings are very green. My garden is divine and is regularly visited by a crazy cockatoo and by little marmoset monkeys who come over for lunch every day." If one project could summarize Lucia's philosophy, it would be the huge, rustic '"bush rope" chandelier that she and her friend Mendonça decorated with flowers and wire, creating a temporary home for three small live birds. The commission was for the launch of a childrenswear label, and at the end of the party the birds were released in a nearby children's park. Just as nature intended…
www.luciamilan.com

"This entrance design for a wedding at the Jockey Club in São Paulo had to make an impression. For the vase on the table we opted for a classical arrangement in bright colours, using pink and green hydrangeas, roses, snapdragons, alstroemerias and green foliage. We also built a 'runway' under the high ceiling with local palm trees, creating a natural atmosphere but increasing the impact."

"*For a wedding (these pages and overleaf) at the
Leopolldo – one of the most renowned venues in
São Paulo – I had total freedom to create the elegance
and warmth requested by the bride. The tables
were either mirrored or laid with black cloth, and
there were elegant but homely touches of silver and
gold throughout via candlesticks, picture frames,
boxes and other objects. My first inspiration was
to use a variety of green leaves and textures; I then
added touches of burgundy. I used old hydrangeas,
amaranthus, tropical maracas, dracaena and
magnolia leaves, annatto seeds, redcurrant and
Sharry Baby orchids. In separate arrangements
I used exotic burgundy orchids to give a sophisticated
mood. The final effect exceeded all expectations.*"

"I made this arrangement in a large glass container: a wild piece of nature confined to a space that's enclosed, yet transparent and open at the top, where the display 'grows' out. I like the contrast between the clean vase and the rustic flowers, like an artwork framed in a museum, or an object found in a laboratory. The arrangement is made like a hand-tied bouquet, but it's cut very short and stands up by itself. Water covers the bottom just enough to feed the plants, which are French tulips, dark calla lilies, pale pink ranunculus, wax flowers, Queen Anne's lace umbels, alliums, millets, panicum grass, coral ferns, scabiosa and Alchemilla mollis."

MARTIN REINICKE
DENMARK

The day Martin Reinicke bought his flower shop in Copenhagen, he told a friend, "There will always be flowers in my life." Blomsterskuret ("Flower Shed") certainly has all the attributes of a humble shed – baskets, wooden crates and tin buckets, all overflowing with exquisite farm-fresh flowers – but it is definitely not ordinary, its natural décor framed by striking dark walls: country simplicity meets urban chic. "I'm self-taught when it comes to flowers," says Martin, "but I've studied architecture, ceramics and the art of decorating, I've sold furniture, and I have my own pottery line. It all comes down to my passion for creating 'rooms'. That's what fuels my artistry, whether arranging furnishings or designing spaces within floral arrangements." Each composition is a delicate orchestration of plants: each finds its place and function, as if Martin's intention was to create ravishing mini-ecosystems of his own imagination. "To work with flowers is to work with something so perfect that the biggest challenge is not to overdo it," he notes. "I barely alter the material, and I avoid constructions. Nature is wholesome, and so easy to destroy, so I apply more respect and less will, and immerse myself wholly in the creative process." However, there is one thing on which Martin still keeps a tight grip: his strong sense of aesthetics. "I try to put my 'beauty spell' on everything, so that I'm still totally in charge of how it looks. I'm a visual artist, a passionate advocate of how anything can be made to look great, amusing, interesting or unusual, instead of dull or ugly." Martin works closely with his customers on their commissions, but his starting point is always a flower, branch or leaf. "I usually work my way through the piece, so I don't know what the finished look will be beforehand. I'm like an abstract painter. I don't do sketches; it all pours out of my mind. The key word is 'celebration'… of life, one might add!"
www.blomsterskuret.dk

"I'VE BECOME MORE CASUAL AND RELAXED ABOUT THE WAY I CREATE ARRANGEMENTS. I TRY TO MAKE THE FLOWERS 'TELL' ME WHAT THEY WANT. IT'S AN ATTEMPT TO USE LESS CONTROL IN MY CREATIVE PROCESS."

"*I like to bring nature into an urban environment, with its combination of hard concrete, glass, bricks and 'trash' on the one hand and weeds, herbs, vegetables and of course wild flowers on the other. This mix holds great appeal for many urbanites, myself included. The tightly bound arrangement above – a little fantasy in a vintage pitcher – was shot in my backyard in the centre of Copenhagen. The base is like a forest floor, with different textures adjacent to each other, while the upper part represents spring flowers that grow in the forest. The arrangement includes poppies at different stages, a lotus pod, Queen Anne's lace umbels, fritillaria, budding spiraea branches, a viburnum snowball, coral ferns and galax leaves.*"

"This tightly bound little bouquet in a vintage earthenware vase consists of artichokes, Alchemilla mollis, alliums, hortensia, Queen Anne's lace umbels, a couple of tiny red grasses and some quince branches poking out of the top. The piece is very rustic and autumnal. I love the season of harvests of fruits and berries and pre-winter vegetables, such as cabbage beets and turnips. It's the time of year when nature gives us food – in deep, burnished colours – to store for winter."

"*This detail from my shop shows fuzzy lime green asparagus fern hanging next to a lantern. Begonias are reflected in the mirror, next to some budding camellias. A basketful of hellebores sits next to one of my own pots, which houses a crassula. Rough iron brackets support weathered wood that was salvaged from a barn construction company near my summerhouse. I love bringing almost brutal materials indoors, to represent the beauty and harshness of nature outside.*"

MAURICE HARRIS
BLOOM & PLUME
USA

"Aromatic greens can elevate even simple arrangements, so fresh garden herbs factor heavily in my work: there's nothing more romantic. Featured above are yellow garden roses with bay leaves and geodes."

I f you were to have Bloom & Plume organize the flowers for your wedding or any other event, you would beg Maurice Harris – owner and florist extraordinaire – to join the party. This effervescent dandy aesthete has an immaculate sense of style. "I would say one of my defining traits is my eye," he admits. "I'm always looking for the thing that no one else is paying attention to, and I bring out its true beauty." His opulent yet restrained displays conjure up a dreamy sensuality and neoclassical-style romanticism. "You're bound to find a feather – or plume – somewhere, and lately I've been using herbs as an unexpected treatment for greenery," he notes. "Shape also plays a big part. You'll usually see a low centre and long sides." With a creative milliner grandmother who was also a florist, Maurice had an early role model. He went on to study fine art and fashion design at Otis College of Art and Design in Los Angeles, before working in the display departments of Barneys New York in Beverly Hills and later Juicy Couture. "Both these experiences helped me to apply my ideas of taste through different filters, which translates to how I work with customers and bring their ideas to life. I also learned a lot about logistics, which is a huge part of the business." Maurice, astonishingly, has been working seriously with flowers for less than a decade. His approach is to source interesting components based on the container and greenery that will form the foundation of an arrangement; one flower is then selected as "the lead singer". "At Barneys," he recalls, "our boss always emphasized that we should let a garment do what it wants to do. The same principle applies to flowers." As for ambition, Maurice shoots for the stars. He would love to be the flower director for "one of the Met balls or an haute couture show … though my secret dream is to do the presentations for ballerinas at the end of a performance, or for winners of pageants!" *www.bloomandplume.com*

"COLOUR, TEXTURE, SHAPE AND SCALE ARE ALL THINGS THAT NEED TO BE PERFECTLY BALANCED. I ALSO LIKE TO GO FOR JUXTAPOSITION, SO YOU'LL OFTEN FIND SOMETHING SOFT AND DELICATE, LIKE A PEONY, NEXT TO SOMETHING A LITTLE BIT MORE DANGEROUS, LIKE A THISTLE. FINDING THIS BALANCE IS THE HARDEST PART."

"Many of my arrangements are rooted in a classic floral vocabulary but, by mixing unlikely materials and exploding traditional shapes, they reference the past without being stuck in it. The plants here include white roses and Silver Dollar eucalyptus."

"*I think all-green arrangements can be extremely sophisticated. By playing with texture and volume, greens can become even more compelling than flower-based arrangements. Included here are Silver Dollar eucalyptus, hydrangea, bay leaf and trachelium.*"

"Part of the joy of flower arranging is discovery. I like an arrangement to give an overall impression but to contain surprising and subtle elements that reveal themselves only after more careful consideration. Included here are heirloom hydrangeas, local hydrangeas, sedum and celosia."

"I enjoy using different varieties of one flower in multiple hues as the foundation for an arrangement. Like a meditation on a theme, colour-family and shape provide a structure from which I like to build. Included here are Faith roses and mint."

"I LIKE TO DRAW THE EYE IN WITH A BOLD STATEMENT, BUT THEN CONTINUE TO ENGAGE WITH MORE SUBTLE DETAILS. WHEN YOU'RE LOOKING AT ONE OF MY ARRANGEMENTS, I WANT YOU TO BE ABLE TO SEE NEW THINGS EACH TIME YOU COME BACK TO IT."

Appreciating the inherent beauty of objects, and enhancing their qualities to make them even more beautiful, is a sublime aspect of everyday life that seems to be ingrained in the Japanese psyche. In effect, this is Mitsunori Hosonuma's philosophy, and it is one he puts into practice on a grand scale. "It is vital to express the beauty of flowers themselves and not to constrain them into something they're not," he states. Under the brand name Hanahiro, Mitsunori has stores in central Tokyo, Osaka and Fukuoka, and a new branch in Hawaii, all dedicated to conveying their owner's singular vision. Mitsunori was himself born into a family of florists, but he also trained in London and Paris, and has been careful to shape his career so that he can indulge in his other great love – travel. His company has been in business for over twenty-five years, weathering constant challenges. "Flowers are expensive in Japan," he notes. "Distribution, staff and fuel costs are huge." Nevertheless he has forged his mini-empire by adapting to circumstances. "The trend used to be about mixing various species and colours in one single arrangement, but now it's about 'simple is best'." For each project Mitsunori is the guide, sourcing unique vases along the way; his loyal team executes his ideas. "We work on numerous weddings, with all the varied requests from brides and grooms; we also do parties and receptions, including one recently for a famous kabuki actor and another for a soccer superstar. It has all shaped me into what I am today: a composer-cum-manager." Comfortable with the concept of "wabi-sabi", the compassionate aesthetic view that beauty is imperfect, Mitsunori states, "I can make an arrangement with one flower or one leaf," but he will also try out new trends ("I was nervous when I used a diamond rose for the first time"). His talent, hard work and ambition have paid off and made him one of Japan's most admirable floral entrepreneurs.

www.hanahiro.jp

"My flagship store in Tokyo's Marunouchi district, a very sophisticated shopping area. The concept here is flowers for daily personal use, gifts for special people, and novelties for brand new customers."

MITSUNORI HOSONUMA
HANAHIRO
JAPAN

215

"I ALWAYS START TO WORK AT THE LAST MINUTE.
I DON'T SKETCH; I PLAN EVERYTHING IN MY MIND,
SO IT'S CONSTANTLY RACING WITH EVER-CHANGING
DESIGNS. THE ART OF FLORAL DECORATION ISN'T
SIMPLY ABOUT CREATING SOMETHING FIGURATIVE.
I BELIEVE FLOWERS MUST CONVEY FEELINGS."

*"Decorating the lobby of the Mandarin
Oriental hotel in Tokyo in early
summer calls for large branches and
brightly coloured flowers. I always
think that arrangements in an area
where a lot of people will gather need
to be fresh and to have great impact."*

"For this wedding reception, the concept for the couple's table (below) centred on white flowers – lilies, roses and lithianthus – together with some greens and a little purple. The most popular colour for floral decorations in Japan is white. The wedding centrepieces (opposite) could be tall, as the hotel had very high ceilings. We used long glass vases and long branches. The large-scale decorations were intended to impress the guests when they entered the room."

"*This arrangement includes king protea, magnolia, succulent flower, lecadendron, veronica, football mums, roses, geranium foliage and pampas grass. A customer ordered it for his wife to celebrate their anniversary. The colours and feel were in the same vein as their wedding had been, several years before.*"

MORGAN PERRONE
VALLEY FLOWER COMPANY
USA

I If you ever stumble upon a scattering of rose petals on the pavements of White River Junction in Vermont, I urge you to stop, as you will have arrived at 93 Gates Street, the headquarters of Valley Flower Company. Enter and meet Morgan Perrone, the self-styled "quirky" owner. "Old women who are covered in costume jewelry and wear funny hats are my unsung heroes," she laughs. Her own skilful use of shape and colour to create unconventional inflections in her floral arrangements certainly defines an appealing style that exalts the potential of any flower chosen. "As a rule, I never follow the rules," she states. "I work fairly quickly, as a lot of the time customers are standing right in front of me, so I tend to work in the moment and I find those arrangements to be the best." Morgan grew up playing in the woods and building forts in tall grasses. "I've always been surrounded by nature," she confirms. "I remember being very young watching bees travel back and forth between the blooms on a raspberry bush in our backyard and marvelling at how intricate the flowers were." Her aim as a florist is to create compositions that are naturalistic, honest and a little imperfect. "I like looking at an arrangement and knowing that nobody has manipulated the flowers to be something they're not. I enjoy it when flowers are just left to be flowers," she remarks. But though light-hearted and easy in her personality and approach, she always remains focused and professional. "A lot of people think that being a florist is 'relaxed' – or, even worse, a hobby – but what we do is hard work, and to do it well you need real passion and dedication. People are relying on you to translate a thought into a visual medium, and that is an extremely challenging job." When asked what her next ambition is, Morgan replies, with a big smile, "To get a full night's sleep and take a vacation."
www.valleyflowercompanyvt.com

221

"*These wedding pieces were made for a couple who wanted to combine his Hindu culture with her New England roots. The textures, colours and flowers were specifically picked to hint towards cultural preferences as well as traditions. We used dahlias, garden roses, pampas grass, hanging amaranths, pieris, marigolds, crocosmia, scabiosa pods, seasonal berries and greenery.*"

*"This arrangement was made for the entrance table at a family party. The customer asked for something fun and casual, with rustic elements. We used **Pink Mink** and **Pin Cushion** proteas, campanula, ranunculus, anemones, hypericum berries, rice flowers and seasonal greenery."*

*"These arrangements were made for a
corporate awards banquet. The organizers
were hoping for something elegant, yet
springy and appropriate to the time of year.
We used stock, dusty miller, hyacinths,
thistles, hydrangeas and trachelium."*

NAZNEEN JEHANGIR
LIBELLULE
INDIA

The graphic image of brightly coloured flowers, placed in sleek monochrome containers against a backdrop of anthracite cement, is best defined by an oxymoron: "tough delicacy". Nazneen Jehangir, the creator of these striking compositions, notes: "A touch of grey is such a grounding element, although I also love lush abundance. I used to be very averse to colour and structure, but now I use plenty of both." Her shop, Libellule, located inside the stylish Le Mill concept store in Mumbai, is a sublime open box in a polished concrete foyer. The pared-down industrial vibe, large black-framed windows, Vasarely-style geometric floor and open ceiling exude cool luxury. Each arrangement ends up looking like an artwork in a modern gallery, although Nazneen is in fact inspired by a different art form: "I used to train as a classical dancer," she explains. "Lines, restraint and elegance are also part of floral design. As in dance, the art should look effortless but belie great thought and work underneath." Nazneen's experiences as a tour operator, and as owner of the event-design company Dragonfly, have also proved invaluable. "I'm good with logistics, and that helps greatly in an industry that requires a lot of shuffling to ensure the best prices and use of perishable products. Paying attention to detail has also helped train and develop my eye." Floral art is still nascent in India, and this brings challenges. "A lot of flowers that are common in Europe have not even been heard of here, so we have to import, and the carbon footprint generated is not something to be taken lightly. However, we are working more and more to see what we can do to grow locally with a global eye. We want to promote indigenous seasonal blooms such as tuberose, jasmine, ramban grass, lotus pods and banana flowers." Libellule is at the forefront of transforming attitudes: "At one of my first exhibitions, a man came up to me and said he'd been dragged there by his wife but had never imagined that something like flowers could be so engaging and moving." Nazneen continues to dream big: "I have this fantasy of creating a hybrid rose named 'Libellule'." Her enthusiasm is infectious, and she and her team are doubtless poised for a blossoming future.
www.libellule.in

"*I stumbled upon the brass tea jar above at Chor Bazaar ('Thieves Market') in Mumbai. Its gritty exterior is softened by the hydrangea, ribbon grass, galopina and fragrant hyacinth within. Above right is a display made for an exhibition called 'Water Bearers'. Collaborators were invited to source typical Indian objects – like this milk measuring ladle – then release them from their original purpose, thus demonstrating that there is beauty in everyday things. The ladle has been filled with village roses, alstroemeria and Xanadu philodendron.*"

"*The delightful buttermilk churn above contains Aranthera Anne Black orchids. The kerosene can on the left – another find from Chor Bazaar – contains liliums, eremurus and an indigenous betel-nut vine called* Supari bhel. *The powder-coated milk cans opposite – tangible expressions of modern Indian urban design, and also included in the 'Water Bearers' exhibition – feature forsythia, eremurus, bouvardia and proteas.*"

"I love copper and its burnished warmth. We found a small hardware store run by a very charming man in the by-lanes of Mumbai and 'cannibalized' various copper pipes to fashion these 'radiator' vases filled with Blue Magic irises and orchids."

"We used multiple fragrant strands of spider lily and marigold to create an entryway for an Indian wedding. Entryways are considered important even if they are at a venue rather than a home, as they signify a welcoming into a family. Indeed, welcome ceremonies are often performed at the gate itself."

OLIVER FERCHLAND
GERMANY

The longer one looks at Oliver Ferchland's compositions, the more sculptural his work appears. His carefully crafted structures either surge like organic trophies or swell like enigmatic vessels. "For me, floral design is a crossover of different areas of interest," he remarks. "That's why I work mostly – but not exclusively – with flowers. There are so many other great materials and forms of expression. I've used bean sprouts for bridal bouquets, Plexiglas plates as a water supply for wild flowers, and raw steel in window dressing. Above all, I'm into construction, with or without flowers." Oliver finds particular inspiration in architecture and nature, especially microbiology. He always wanted to work in a creative industry, and when a schoolboy of only 14 he joined an apprenticeship programme, which took him to a flower shop. "I ended up spending every free minute there until I graduated from junior high school," he recalls. He later ventured into fashion design, and this informs his work to this day, in the form of floral dresses and one particular wedding dress made entirely out of white paper. "But I experienced a significant shift in my way of working when I attended the German national florist championship a few years ago. Preparing for that competition, I developed a more naturalistic style of construction and everything fell into place." Several awards later, Oliver has enjoyed commissions that include the decorations for a royal wedding in Bahrain as well as the more usual seasonal designs and event-led corporate arrangements that are his staple. Designing conceptually, he first identifies a core idea or material, then works on several experimental ideas at the same time in order to define the final outcome. When it is time to add the finishing touches, it is immediately clear to him whether elements are destined to look at each other or to turn away – "the exact moment when you recognize that everything is as it should be; I always say that flowers should 'dance' and be free". This Oliver achieves with distinction. His compositions always have an air of stop-motion about them, as if he has frozen time and captured grace in action.

www.facebook.com/oliver.ferchland.3

"The development of this piece mixed the concept of a cornfield with that of an organ. The rhythmic sequence of flowers was intended to give the impression of deliberate composition. Included are dried wheat, alliums, Sandersonia, gloriosa, viburnum, zinnias, dianthus, cotinus, anethum, alstroemeria, ammi, Asparagus asparagoides, phytolacca and blackberry."

"A PIECE IS USUALLY COMPLETELY OUTLINED IN MY MIND BEFORE I START MAKING IT, BUT NATURE IS FULL OF SURPRISES AND SOMETIMES A MATERIAL BRINGS SOMETHING SO UNIQUE AND UNEXPECTED THAT I VEER FROM MY INITIAL PLAN AND ALLOW MYSELF TO FREE-FLOW."

"I've always been interested in the depiction of objects in art. Large-scale pieces can create an atmosphere of their own in a room. The homemade 'vase' opposite is in the form of a disc projecting from a central axis. The lateral projection gives the body its own special dynamism. This form of container should appear like an island hovering in the room, carrying a forest of flowers (detail above), so I used weighty materials that appear to defy the laws of gravity. Included are lathyrus, phytolacca, dianthus, cotinus, phlox, lysimachia, ammi, rhodochiton, achillea, oncidium and blackberry."

"*With this arrangement it was important for me to create a positive effect of sheer joy. Expressive floral forms such as gloriosa were intended to enhance the strong colours.* Zinnias, steel grass, Sandersonia, gerberas, dill, dianthus, helichrysum *and* Asparagus asparagoides *were also used.*"

"This piece is an object in itself, the aim being to create the impression that the tendrils are winding round the sides of the plants, as if reaching out to give themselves breathing space. The free movement of the structure is also meant to emphasize its independence from any rigidly imposed form. Flowers used include oncidium orchids, steel grass, anthurium, alliums, lunaria, blackberry, phytolacca and bear grass."

REBECCA LOUISE LAW

UK

"I LOVE THE CHALLENGE OF WORKING WITH A PERISHABLE, DELICATE, LIVING MATERIAL; THE FACT THAT YOU HAVE ONE CHANCE TO GET IT RIGHT. ROSES MAY BE MY FAVOURITE: THEY HAVE SO MANY COLOURS TO WORK WITH, I LOVE THEIR FRAGRANCE ... AND THORNS ARE BEAUTIFUL."

Flowers are the archetypal elements favoured by artists who wish to question concepts of life and death. Rebecca Louise Law is among them, and her ambition is to demonstrate that every stage of a flower's life span should be appreciated. "My work is perceived as a challenging view of beauty through the use of dying flowers," she notes. "Some people say it's awe-inspiring, which is humbling." Living on Columbia Road in East London, which hosts a famous weekly flower market, Rebecca fills her home with living, dead and artificial flowers, and has hung large paintings of flowers on most of the walls. She lives and breathes flowers, and it turns out she was born into it. "Over six generations of my family have been gardeners," she reveals. "My grandmother and aunt also painted flowers and encouraged me to do the same, and my father is head gardener of a National Trust property and an amazingly creative natural artist." Rebecca traces her decision to be a floral artist back to her university days, when, while studying fine art, she "replaced paint with flowers". She went on to become senior floral designer at McQueens (see p. 170), where she learned valuable lessons in business management and luxury event planning. She now operates out of a studio in Hackney and enjoys experimenting with materials and ideas, including using copper wire to suspend arrangements ("it contrasts beautifully with drying flowers") and featuring birdsong in installations. Notable commissions have included a "Hanging Garden" for Hermès at the Royal Opera House in London – "seven thousand flowers, forty varieties, twenty staff, twenty hours, and months of planning" – and she received a standing ovation at the opening of her "Roses" installation at the Garden Museum in London. As she says, "I ultimately want as many people as possible to experience flowers physically." Her sensory floral walls and skies, encouraging onlookers to become active participants in her works, are truly unforgettable.

www.rebeccalouiselaw.com

"The piece opposite was made for a solo exhibition at The Tavern Gallery in Cambridge, England. It was an installation of mixed flowers hanging from a chandelier."

"Artists from all over Europe gathered to create 'Ecoart in Landscape', a project aiming to encourage tourism through art in Abruzzo, Italy. Working in the Anversa commune and representing England, I collaborated with Heddy Castberg, who was representing Norway. Together we made 'The Arch' with deadwood and lichen gathered from the forest floor of the national park in Abruzzo."

"'The Nest' was made as part of a project with two objectives: to encourage inner-city children to engage with nature and natural materials, and to connect children from mainstream schools and special schools through art. I worked with children from St Philips Primary School and The Granta School on four pieces of land art. All of our pieces were made with deadwood and moss, gathered from the forest floor of Hoe Fen at Anglesey Abbey."

"For the 'Floriculture' exhibition at the Garden Museum in London, which explored the Kenyan rose industry and Fair Trade roses, I designed a site-specific installation using donated materials, including 3,500 roses from the New Covent Garden Flower Market. Each was hung from copper wire, which was attached to a steel frame structure."

SARA JOHANSSON
SWEDEN

"For this arrangement I used varieties of tulip, rose, hydrangea, lisianthus, chrysanthemum and carnation. Mixing the different shades of pink and the different shapes of flower makes the structure harmonious. It's a romantic composition that's appropriate for most occasions. I often make such arrangements for the hotels I work with."

S ara Johansson's parents had all the signs their five-year-old daughter would become one of Sweden's most acclaimed floral designers when she started to give them little bunches of flowers she had hand-picked on her way home from school. She never lost her passion. "As a teenager, I spent time in the shop of a fantastic florist, who made me believe in myself and encouraged me to apply to the prestigious school in Norrköping, from which I graduated with honours." Sara's current work, while using the sophisticated methodology that comes with the maturity of a full-fledged designer, seems to have maintained a fresh touch redolent of childhood innocence. "I've now worked in this profession for over twenty years," she says. "I opened my own shop and have grown to become a florist with a lot of audacious ideas – my trademark. My biggest achievement to date is to have organized the flowers for all the ceremonies held at the City Hall for the past ten years: a great honour." In addition, Sara has supplied the floral arrangements for the Stockholm Water prize on numerous occasions. She credits her love of floral craft to the fact that there are no limits in terms of shape, colour or material. "Every flower is different, so no two arrangements can be exactly the same. The sky is really the limit. I think around the clock about flowers and the multitude of options for arranging them." But, regardless of how lavish or theatrical a work can be, Sara hankers after creations that hold an immediate appeal – a simple connection to the heart. She understands the language of flowers, living as she does in a home surrounded by them, whether outdoors (her garden) or inside (her bedroom and bathroom are filled with vases). "Each season brings a flower that's a little more special to me than others. In the spring I covet mini irises and grape hyacinths, in the summer I indulge in peonies and garden roses, and autumn allows me to gather chrysanthemums, which come in a myriad of forms." Sara looks up to talents such as Tage Andersen in Denmark, Gregor Lersch in Germany and Paula Pryke in the UK, but she should know that she is a major source of inspiration, too.

www.personligablomster.se
www.personligablomster.wordpress.com

"*I also like working with multiple small arrangements. Here I used carnations in various shades of purple and pink, and countered this with bright orange gerberas, gloriosa and asparagus fern to produce strong contrasts. I like to make round compact forms on top of which you can build irregular shapes to create really beautiful works of art.*"

SARAH WINWARD HONEY OF A THOUSAND FLOWERS

USA

"I'M OFTEN INSPIRED BY ONE FLOWER AND TAKE CUES FROM ITS COLOUR AND SHAPE TO CHOOSE THE FLOWERS TO GO WITH IT, AND I BUILD THE ARRANGEMENT AROUND IT. THE SECOND FLOWER USUALLY HAS A BIG ROLE IN DECIDING THE DIRECTION OF THE ARRANGEMENT; IT'S THE 'FORK IN THE ROAD'. THE REST PLAY IMPORTANT PARTS WITH ACCENT COLOUR OR TEXTURE. THE SMALL BITS THAT I ADD TOWARDS THE END COMPLETE THE LOOK."

Working with flowers may have surprising similarities to early parenthood. "As a mother," says Sarah Winward, "you hold your baby tight, you smell them, and you study every part of them because you know soon they will grow up. I think the time I spend with flowers is similarly intense because I'm trying to enjoy every bit of them while I can." This self-taught and much sought-after floral designer from Salt Lake City is creative to the core. Her path to success, however, was not a straight one. She studied Middle Eastern and International Relations, after falling in love with the Arabic language. Then she worked in customer services in the floral industry, which was not for her. But once she'd helped a few friends plan the décor and flowers for their weddings, she started arranging flowers for herself and never stopped. She got the name for her business during a trip to Morocco. "My husband and I visited a beekeeper who transports his bees up and down the Atlas mountains so that they create flavoured honey from whatever is blooming in a particular area: we tried his orange blossom honey, thyme honey and cactus honey. When we told him we also kept bees, he asked what flavour of honey they made. I didn't know the word for 'wild' in Arabic, so explained that our bees extract nectar from all of the flowers around our home, as there isn't one heavy crop of anything because we live in a city. He said that in Arabic they call this 'honey of a thousand flowers'. I knew instantly it had to be my business name. The more I think about it, the more I feel like it describes my work. My work is a reflection of everything around me, both in literal terms, referring to the flowers I use, and in more metaphorical ways, referring to everything that has made me who I am." Flowers in their natural state inspire Sarah the most. "I live at the base of the Rocky Mountains; I also have an ample-sized garden that I let run wild." This confident creator, who loves to work hard under pressure ("my biggest strength and my biggest weakness"), continues to surpass all expectations with her own unbridled naturalistic flair.

www.sarahwinward.com

"This arrangement includes ranunculus, Quicksand roses, jasmine vine, thistle and calcynia. The palette was inspired by the subtle variations in colour between all the focal flowers. The earthy cream and mauve tones gently fade from one tone to the next."

"*The arrangement on the right, with its feminine colours and delicate textures, features ranunculus, sweet peas, clematis, scabiosa and maidenhair fern. The combination is wild, inspired by the late months of spring and early summer, when the entire valley is starting to burst with flowers. Below is an arrangement that uses the Japanese maple as its base. In the late summer months the small leaves of the Japanese maple, perfectly positioned on tiered branches, have the most beautiful rich green colour to them. The other blooms in the arrangement include foxgloves, campanula, rose and jasmine vine, as well as heuchera foliage from my garden. Opposite is a composition that consists of some of my favourite early spring delicacies: hellebores, ranunculus, fritillaria and cherry blossom. Spring is full of tiny blooms with a lot of intricate detail to them, such as speckled petals and ornate stamens.*"

258

"The undertones of many spring flowers have an earthy hue to them. I think these lend themselves to very sophisticated, moody compositions as well as the usual cheerful, bright spring arrangements. This design includes spray roses, fritillaria, ranunculus, cherry blossom, spiraea, hellebores and passion vine."

261

"Poppies are the most cheerful of flowers. Sometimes you can't compete with them, so I let them be on their own. In this arrangement, papaver poppies from Italy are accented with grape ivy. I let them go wild in a vintage champagne bucket."

"*This arrangement features the lush blooms of summer in mouthwatering berry tones. Garden roses, dahlias, clematis and jasmine vine: I imagine these being perfectly fitting in a garden setting, looking as if they went straight from the earth to the vase.*"

SASKIA DE VALK
VLINDER&VOGEL
THE NETHERLANDS

"Late summer organic flowers, individually selected to be exhibited and examined. These blooms are in the unconscious memory of the Dutch people: smelled, picked and seen growing in their granny's garden. The pinks are dahlia, cosmos, zinnia and Nostalgia rose; the oranges are kniphofia and calendula."

Floral arrangements that appeal to the spirit through the senses are Saskia de Valk's speciality. Her compositions are nothing short of angelic: delicate visual metaphors for what she calls "Daily Beauty", or "how to make something beautiful out of something ordinary, like inserting long stems of cow parsley into a field bouquet, with air and space between each component and no unnecessary foliage". This approach goes hand-in-hand with Saskia's advocacy of urban farming practices, organic flower-growing and recycling: "I sew dead flowers onto canvas with gold thread, or dry them in small vases, or give them to artists who make photo projects with them or just compost them in their garden." Saskia was first introduced to the world of flowers when she was asked to lend a hand at her favourite organic flower stall. "I fell in love with creating bouquets, and eventually settled in a flower shop." In 2010, she launched a web shop with

a graphic designer friend, curating all kinds of beautiful Nature-related things. "Our first commission was to do a presentation of our shop at a design event. We didn't have enough products to show, so decided to make a floral scape with all the flowers that were in bloom around Amsterdam at the time," she recalls. "We displayed the flowers in hundreds of laboratory vessels, arranged by colour gradient. It looked fantastic, and I think it coincided with the moment I really experienced the power of the flower." A year later Saskia established Vlinder&Vogel ("Butterfly&Bird"), selling handmade objects, such as the Bloemenlab II, a wall vase made out of a laboratory vessel and accommodating one small flower, as well as flowers to order. It comes as no surprise to discover that Saskia listens to classical music while she crafts, and that she identifies with the work of choreographer and dancer Pina Bausch. "She often made use of basic resources: in *Nelken* her dancers perform in a huge field of carnations, and in *Sacre du Printemps* they perform on real red earth." In Saskia's works, too, an exceptional purity radiates and time feels magically suspended.
www.vlinderenvogel.com

"This little vignette shows (from top) my sketchbook, with a marigold; some colour research using tape, a marigold and a carnation; a jam jar acting as a bell jar, containing a cutting; a little note; a home-made tincture of marigold; and dahlia petals for colour research purposes."

"In the 'Still Life of White Cosmos and Scabiosa in the Glasshouse' opposite, a bright simple flower is captured in all its pure beauty. To the left is an arrangement of organic flowers – Anethum graveolens, rose and marigold – picked in the fields at the height of spring. Below is an installation on a table designed to offer light, space and brightness, giving the flowers the best platform to show off their individual shapes and colours."

"SIMPLICITY, DURABILITY AND BEAUTY CAN ALL GO TOGETHER. IN WINTER I WORK MOSTLY WITH BRANCHES AND 'STILLNESS'. IN SUMMER I CAN DRIVE HOME FROM THE LOCAL ORGANIC FARMS WITH A CAR FULL OF FRAGRANT FLOWERS, WHICH I WILL USE TO CREATE SOMETHING BEAUTIFUL AND TO SHARE MY HAPPINESS WITH OTHER PEOPLE."

"During the summer, I harvest flowers, mainly dahlias, from our organic garden. I feel so close to nature, its smells and calm sounds. Opposite is a 'Dahlia Still Life': a love affair between an object and a flower, made for Elle Decoration *magazine."*

SEAN COOK
MR. COOK
AUSTRALIA

An abstract stain, as when wet daubs of watercolour merge on paper, greets one with hallucinatory power. And that's just the business card and logo. The Mr.COOK store in Double Bay, Sydney, is even more stunning: part modern, part rustic, with lavish shelves of exotic flowers and a wooden bench that can be split and moved around to transform the configuration of the space. The owner, Sean Cook, credits his obsession with flowers to his grandmother. "In her fern/orchid house, there wasn't a spare space on the benches or walls," he recalls, "and she had a wonderful garden." His own aesthetic flair is striking. "All my friends will tell you I adore a bit of pink, in all shades from fluoro to blush. I'm also obsessed with anything scented, especially tuberose, gardenias and columbines, which are scarce here." His first job, as a visual merchandiser, led him to work for an event production company, which provided great experience in logistics and production, but "it wasn't until I started to work with Saskia Havekes at Grandiflora that I really discovered what could be done". Sean's first big commission was for a fiftieth birthday party in the middle of winter in Thredbo. "The only brief was that it had to be masculine," he recounts. The project involved two trucks and a van full of materials and florists. "We took driftwood from Lake Jindabyne and suspended a 'river' of it from the ceiling of the marquee, with clusters of orange banksias attached, and we did other large installations throughout." The preparations took three days, but the client was ecstatic. Now, after nearly two decades in the industry, Sean is renowned for his bold, eclectic and colourful compositions, and has established strong relationships with both suppliers and customers. "I've had brides and their mothers cry from happiness when they saw their bridal flowers," he sighs. Whether it's your big day or not, Sean's work is bound to work its magic on you.
www.mrcook.com.au

"We shot the arrangements on these pages and overleaf at Elements I Love, one of my favourite stores in Sydney. I found these incredible French doors, and my photographer and I decided it would be great to do two floral pieces either side of the glass. Dahlias were at their best, so I had the idea of giving the shots an autumnal feel, with one side stronger in colour and the other more muted. I love lots of texture, so I incorporated green amaranthus, trailing passion vine, callicarpa and quince. I also brought Hugo, my little Quaker parrot (above), as I thought his colouring would be perfect against the autumn hydrangea. He was such a good little model!"

272

"MY STYLE IS REFLECTED IN MY WORK, HOME AND SHOP. I LIKE TO ENHANCE NATURAL FORMS THROUGH TONAL ARRANGEMENTS AND LOTS OF TEXTURE AND LAYERING. AS FAR AS INSPIRATION GOES, I LOVE EVERYTHING FROM THE OLD WEATHERED OREGON TIMBER IN MY SHOP TO THE SUPER-HIGH GLOSS OF A DALE FRANK PAINTING."

TRACEY DEEP
FLORAL SCULPTURES
AUSTRALIA

Twigs, branches and seed pods are sewn together with wire mesh and other industrial thrift items in a process that turns often disregarded natural elements into the prime heroes of an artwork. This is salvation through salvage, unearthing beauty in what would otherwise be left to decay and oblivion. Tracey Deep is an artist who happens to use Nature as her medium; the fact that she has access to native Australian plants makes her work all the more striking, resonating as it seems to with the Aboriginal approach to land and spiritual values. Particularly passionate about plays of texture, shape and colour, Tracey states: "I try to create visually balanced pieces that are pleasing to the eye. I enjoy placing a dried element against a fresh element to create that contrast and tonal state of happiness. Most importantly, I add movement to give a piece energy and vibrancy." Her work has naturally evolved as she has mastered her medium. "I've been creating living sculptures for a few decades now, and I've come to enjoy using both organic and industrial elements," she explains. "I'm attracted to pieces that *look* organic but are in fact industrial and have usually had another life. This reworking of the old into something new inspires and feeds my soul." Tracey needs hardly add, "I'm a very passionate, spiritual and soulful person, and I have a very special connection to Mother Nature. I'm a true tree lover and hugger. I think this comes shining through in my work, giving it a special quality that tends to draw people in and leave them touched in some way." Her studio abounds with pots and shelves full of organic curiosities and works-in-progress. She lets her elements speak to her and guide her – a form of improvisation that is nonetheless always galvanized by patterns found in Nature. These emerge in hanging or free-standing sculptural forms, brought to life in the beautiful chaos of a workshop that itself resembles a concentrated, re-composed tract of Australian bush.

floralsculptures@bigpond.com
www.instagram.com/floralsculptures

"*My exhibition 'Spirit' was inspired by a trip to Uluru and Kata Tjuta, huge weather-effected rock formations that survive through extreme temperature conditions and that change colour at every angle and time of day. My spirit was lifted by the beauty and peace of these sacred sites of the indigenous people. I found so much beauty in the silence, scale and contrasting colour palettes. It inspired my show, which involved working with organic and industrial found material, reworked and transformed into something totally new.*"

"The piece opposite is from my exhibition 'Dreaming', and was made with stems of honesty. The work was inspired by the lightness, translucence and overall magical look of the material. I love the woody texture of the delicate branches, the luminosity of the fragile seeds, the natural earthy tones, and the whimsical, playful, dream-like qualities the piece seems to bring out. The shadow also adds to the natural imprint of the piece. With the work featured above, my concept was to combine rescued industrial materials, such as rusted steel from a building site and a rice paper blind from landfill, with natural organic materials, in order to breathe new life into them. I seek to make my pieces 'dance'. By working with elements such as flame tree pods gone to seed or dried-out palm fronds and coconut fibres, I aim to accentuate the beauty in Mother Nature's eternal cycle of life."

"My studio in Redfern, with special finds fresh from the flower market and special pieces sourced over the years and used as props. Unusual seed pods, luscious leaves, architectural succulents: all play an inspirational role, as I love to experiment with textures, shapes and colours."

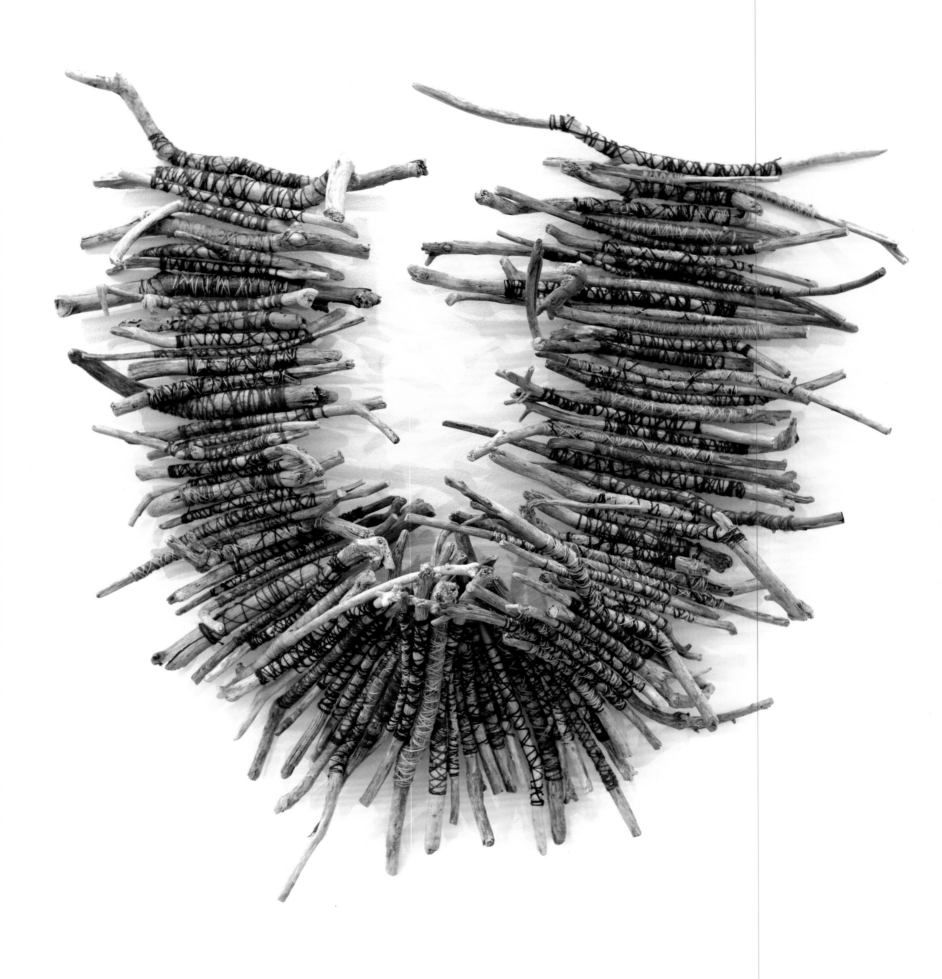

"Opposite is a 'Tree Spirit' piece from my 'Spirit' exhibition. The work was inspired by ghost eucalyptus gum trees and patterns made by Nature. I used cotton string to create patterns on driftwood, hand-weaving them to form shapes, and then hung the piece in the form of a sacred offering; a celebration of the beauty of Mother Nature. Thanks to a generous private collector, it now hangs in a birthing centre for all mothers with their newborns to enjoy. For the piece below I rescued the base of a plant found discarded on the side of a road. A found rusted wire also holds the installation together. Reflecting my love of the underwater world, I used washed-up coral and sea sponges rescued after storms. I added fronds from a succulent plant to create movement, depth and volume."

"WHAT DRIVES ME IS THE CONSTANT SURPRISING DISCOVERY OF NEW THINGS, THE NEVER-ENDING INSPIRATION AND APPRECIATION OF NATURE'S BEAUTY THROUGHOUT THE WHOLE PROCESS, GOING FROM LIVING ORGANIC MATERIAL TO DRYING AND THE ENDING OF LIFE."

A

Aleksandra Schutz
www.facebook.com/pages/
Aleksandra/142269745805357
www.instagram.com/aleksandradiary

Amy Merrick
www.flickr.com/photos/
emersonmerrick
www.twitter.com/emersonmerrick

Andreas Verheijen
www.facebook.com/pages/
Andreas-Verheijen-flower-
engineer/152884198081933

Anna Day & Ellie Jauncey:
THE FLOWER APPRECIATION
SOCIETY
www.facebook.com/pages/
The-Flower-Appreciation-
Society/255664854499032
www.instagram.com/Flowersociety
www.twitter.com/flowersociety

Ariel Dearie:
ARIEL DEARIE FLOWERS
www.facebook.com/pages/
Ariel-Dearie-Flowers/
134129969996700
www.instagram.com/
arieldearieflowers
www.twitter.com/ArielDearie

Azuma Makoto
www.facebook.com/MakotoAzuma
www.twitter.com/azumamakoto

B

Baptiste Pitou
4, rue de l'Abbé Grégoire,
75006 Paris, France
Tel +33 (0) 1 42 84 19 08

Björn Kroner
www.facebook.com/bjorn.kroner
www.facebook.com/jungewilde

C

Caris Haughan &
Vanessa Partridge:
PRUNELLA
www.facebook.com/pages/
Prunella/230779116962857
www.instagram.com/prunellaflowers
www.pinterest.com/prunellaflowers
www.twitter.com/Prunellaflowers
Studio space (weddings and events)
and also pop-up shop for Christmas,
Mothers Day and workshops:
175–177 Mollison Street,
Kyneton 3444,
VIC, Australia
Tel +61 (0) 416 296 433

Clarisse Béraud:
ATELIER VERTUMNE
www.facebook.com/
clarisse.beraud.vertumne
www.facebook.com/pages/
Agence-de-stylisme-floral-
Vertumne/150627495001894
12, rue de la Sourdière,
75001 Paris, France
Tel +33 (0) 1 42 86 06 76

D

Dan Takeda:
DAN TAKEDA FLOWER & DESIGN
www.facebook.com/pages/Dan-Takeda-
Flower-Design/182770601927326

Doctor Lisa Cooper
www.facebook.com/pages/
Doctor-Cooper-Studio/
601947553163615
www.instagram.com/doctorcooper

E

Emily Thompson:
EMILY THOMPSON FLOWERS
www.facebook.com/
EmilyThompsonFlowers
www.instagram.com/
emilythompsonflowers

Erin Benzakein & Family:
FLORET
www.facebook.com/erin.benzakein
www.flickr.com/photos/floretflowers
www.instagram.com/floretflower
www.pinterest.com/floretflwrfarm
www.twitter.com/FloretFlwrFarm

G

Giota Gialleli:
ANTONELLO
24A Skoufa Street, Athens, 10673, Greece
Tel +30 21 0360 8969

H

Harijanto Setiawan:
BOENGA
www.facebook.com/boengaflowers

Heiko Bleuel
Grüneburgweg 88, 60323
Frankfurt am Main, Germany
Tel +49 (0) 69/91 50 88 11

Helena Lunardelli:
ATELIER HELENA LUNARDELLI
www.facebook.com/FlorGentil
www.flickr.com/photos/
atelierhelenalunardelli
www.instagram.com/helenalunardelli

Holly Vesecky &
Rebecca Uchtman:
HOLLYFLORA
www.facebook.com/HollyfloraLA
www.instagram.com/hollyflorala
www.twitter.com/hollyflora

I

Isabel Marías:
ELISABETH BLUMEN
www.facebook.com/pages/
Elisabeth-Blumen/197255316971840
www.instagram.com/elisabethblumen

J

Joan Xapelli:
FLOWERS BY BORNAY
www.facebook.com/flowersbybornay
www.flowersbybornay.tumblr.com

K

Kally Ellis:
MCQUEENS
www.facebook.com/McQueensflowers
www.flickr.com/photos/
mcqueensflowers
www.instagram.com/mcqueensflowers
www.twitter.com/mcqueensflowers
70–72 Old Street, The City,
London EC1V 9AJ, UK
Tel +44 (0) 20 7251 5505

Kristen Caissie:
MOON CANYON DESIGN
www.facebook.com/pages/
Moon-Canyon-Design-Co/
180081525414870
www.instagram.com/mooncanyon
www.pinterest.com/mooncanyon
www.twitter.com/MoonCanyon

L

Lindsey Brown:
LINDSEY MYRA & THE
LITTLE FLOWER FARM
www.facebook.com/
TheUrbanFlowerFarm
www.flickr.com/people/lindseymyra
www.instagram.com/lindseymyra
www.pinterest.com/lindseymyra

Lotte Lawson:
LOTTE & BLOOM
www.facebook.com/lotte.bloom
www.flickr.com/photos/lotteandbloom
www.instagram.com/lotteandbloom
www.twitter.com/lotteandbloom

Lucia Milan
www.facebook.com/pages/Lucia-Milan-Design-Floral/298966546828513
www.instagram.com/luciamilan

M

Martin Reinicke
www.facebook.com/Blomsterskuret
Værnedamsvej 3A, 1819
Frederiksberg C, Denmark
Tel +45 33 21 62 22

Maurice Harris:
BLOOM & PLUME
www.bloomandplume.tumblr.com
www.facebook.com/BloomandPlume
www.instagram.com/bloomandplume

Mitsunori Hosonuma:
HANAHIRO
www.facebook.com/mitsunori.hosonuma
www.facebook.com/pages/Hanahiro
Hanahiro-CQ/342306172521058
List of shops:
www.hanahiro.jp/c50.htm

Morgan Perrone:
VALLEY FLOWER COMPANY
www.facebook.com/
valleyflowercompany
www.instagram.com/valleyflowerco
www.pinterest.com/valleyflowerco
www.twitter.com/valleyflowerco

N

Nazneen Jehangir:
LIBELLULE
c/o Le Mill,
17–25 Nandlal Jani Road,
next to Wadi Bunder
New Railway Bridge,
Wadi Bunder (East), Mumbai, India
Shop: +91 98 70955128
Office: +91 22 22853033

O

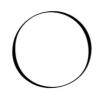

Oliver Ferchland
www.facebook.com/oliver.ferchland.3

R

Rebecca Louise Law
www.twitter.com/RebeccaLLaw

S

Sara Johansson
www.facebook.com/personliga.blomster
www.instagram.com/blomsterbrittan

Sarah Winward:
HONEY OF A THOUSAND FLOWERS
www.facebook.com/pages/
Honey-of-a-Thousand-Flowers-
Sarah-Winward/134125279997651
www.instagram.com/sarah_winward
www.pinterest.com/sarahwinward
www.twitter.com/sarah_winward

Saskia de Valk:
VLINDER&VOGEL
www.facebook.com/
vlinderenvogel

Sean Cook:
MR.COOK
www.facebook.com/MrCookFlowers
www.instagram.com/mrcookflowers
318 New South Head Road,
Double Bay, Sydney,
NSW 2028, Australia
Tel +61 (0) 2 9363 5550

T

Tracey Deep:
FLORAL SCULPTURES
www.instagram.com/floralsculptures
Studio G01, 59 Great Buckingham Street,
Redfern, Sydney, NSW 2016, Australia
Tel +61 (0) 2 9326 9014

p. 2: Foliage and tools for the making of Azuma Makoto's 'Collapsible Leaves' series (see pp. 46–49). Photo Shunsuke Shiinoki, TOUNOKI Co., Ltd.

p. 7: Detail of an arrangement by Dan Takeda of Dan Takeda Flower & Design (see p. 97). Photo Caesar Production (www.caesarproduction.com).

Alexandra Schutz: pp. 9, 12 & 13 by Trish Lee/Tealilyphotography (www.tealilyphotography.com); pp. 10, 11 & portrait p. 284 by Luisa Brimble (www.luisabrimble.com); p. 14 courtesy of Rebecca Jovanova (www.samanthawills.com), photography by Scott Ehler (www.scottehler.com); p. 15 courtesy of Aleksandra Schutz.

Amy Merrick: pp. 16, 17 & portrait p. 284 by Amanda Hakan (www.amandahakan.com); pp. 18, 19, 20 & 21 courtesy of Amy Merrick.

Andreas Verheijen: p. 22 courtesy of Andreas Verheijen; p. 23 by Jan Willem Kaldenbach (www.jwkaldenbach.com); pp. 24 & 25 by Wendelien Daan (www.wendeliendaan.nl); p. 26 portrait of ArtEZ Fashion Design graduate Liselore Frowijn & p. 27 portrait of ArtEZ Fashion Design graduate Pieter Eliëns, both by Louise te Poele (www.louisetepoele.nl); portrait p. 284 by Christopher Bowen (www.christopherbowen.com).

Anna Day & Ellie Jauncey/The Flower Appreciation Society: all photos courtesy of Anna Day & Ellie Jauncey, The Flower Appreciation Society.

Ariel Dearie/Ariel Dearie Flowers: pp. 34, 35 & portrait p. 284 by Bryce Covey (www.brycecoveyphotography.com); pp. 36, 37, 38 & 39 courtesy of Ariel Dearie, Ariel Dearie Flowers.

Azuma Makoto: all photos by Shunsuke Shiinoki, TOUNOKI Co., Ltd.

Baptiste Pitou: all photos by Niels Stoltenborg (www.nielsstoltenborg.com).

Björn Kroner: all photos by Peter Johann Kierzkowski (www.pjk-atelier.de).

Caris Haughan & Vanessa Partridge/Prunella: pp. 80–81 by Simon Griffiths (www.simongriffiths.com.au); pp. 82, 83 & portraits p. 284 by Erin Neale and Tara Pearce (www.erinandtara.com.au); pp. 84–85 by Jesse Hisco (www.jessehisco.com.au); pp. 86 & 87 by Farrah Allan (www.farrahallan.com).

Clarisse Béraud/Atelier Vertumne: pp. 89, 92, 93 & portrait p. 284 courtesy of Clarisse Béraud, Atelier Vertumne; pp. 90–91 by Pascal Baudrier (www.pascalbaudrier.book.fr).

Dan Takeda/Dan Takeda Flower & Design: all photos by Caesar Production (www.caesarproduction.com).

Doctor Lisa Cooper: pp. 102–3 by Eliza Gorka; pp. 104 & 105 by Kylie Coutts (www.kyliecoutts.com), styling by Jolyon Mason @ 2c Artist Management, hair by Jenny Kim @ M.A.P, model: Nick Hall @ London Management, originally published in *Manuscript*, Issue 02; pp. 106, 107 & 108–9 by Robin Hearfield; portrait p. 284 by Joshua Heath (www.joshuaheath.net).

Emily Thompson/Emily Thompson Flowers: pp. 110–11 © Josh Marianelli Photography (www.joshmarianelli.com); pp. 112–13 & 116 by Sophia Moreno-Bunge (www.sophiamorenobunge.com); pp. 114, 115 & 117 courtesy of Emily Thompson, Emily Thompson Flowers; portrait p. 284 by Maria Robledo (www.judycasey.com/photographers/maria-robledo).

Erin Benzakein & Family/Floret: all photos courtesy of Erin Benzakein & Family, Floret.

Giota Gialleli/Antonello: all photos by Manos Spanos (www.manosspanosphotographics.tumblr.com).

Harijanto Setiawan/Boenga: all photos courtesy of Harijanto Setiawan, Boenga.

Heiko Bleuel: all photos by Till Roos (www.tillroos.de).

Helena Lunardelli/Atelier Helena Lunardelli: pp. 145 & 148–9 by Fabio Ribeiro (compotaonline.com.br); pp. 146 & 147 by Gilberto Oliveira Jr. workshop (www.oh-images.com.br); portrait p. 285 by Guilherme Morelli (www.guimorelli.com.br).

Holly Vesecky & Rebecca Uchtman/Hollyflora: all photos by Nancy Neil Photography (www.nancyneil.com).

Isabel Marías/Elisabeth Blumen: pp. 157, 160 & 161 courtesy of Isabel Marías, Elisabeth Blumen; pp. 158 & 159 by Julia Lomo Juno (www.junoproducciones.com); portrait p. 285 by Raúl Córdoba Zamorano (www.raulcordobaphotography.com).

Joan Xapelli/Flowers by Bornay: pp. 162, 163, 164, 165, 167 & portrait p. 285 by Marssal (www.marssal.net); pp. 166 & 168–9 courtesy of Joan Xapelli, Flowers by Bornay

Kally Ellis/McQueens: pp. 170–71, 172, 173, 174 & portrait p. 285 courtesy of Kally Ellis, © McQueens; p. 175 courtesy of Mulberry (www.mulberry.com).

Kristen Caissie/Moon Canyon Design: all photos by Kimberly Geneviève (www.kimberlygenevieve.com).

Lindsey Brown/Lindsey Myra & The Little Flower Farm: all photos courtesy of Lindsey Brown, Lindsey Myra & The Little Flower Farm.

Lotte Lawson/Lotte & Bloom: all photos courtesy of Lotte Lawson, Lotte & Bloom, except for portrait p. 285 by Cara Forbes (www.lillianandleonard.com).

Lucia Milan: pp. 196 & 197 by Alexandre Pirani (www.apiranifotos.blogspot.com); pp. 198, 199, 200 & 201 by Júlia Ribeiro (www.juliaribeiro.net); portrait p. 286 by Gabriel Milan.

Martin Reinicke: all photos by Sara Lindbaek (www.saralindbaek.dk).

Maurice Harris/Bloom & Plume: all photos by Tyson FitzGerald (www.tysonfitzgerald.com).

Mitsunori Hosonuma/Hanahiro: pp. 214–15, 218 & 219 by Mr. Kenichi Fujimoto; pp. 216 & 217 courtesy of Mitsunori Hosonuma, Hanahiro; portrait p. 286 by Ms. Haraeri.

Morgan Perrone/Valley Flower Company: pp. 220, 221, 224, 225, 226–7 & portrait p. 286 by Taylor K. Long; pp. 222 & 223 by Michael Tallman (www.michael-tallman.com).

Nazneen Jehangir/Libellule: all photos courtesy of Nazneen Jehangir, Libellule.

Oliver Ferchland: all photos by Andreas Gruner (Info@andreasgruner.com).

Rebecca Louise Law: pp. 245 & 247 courtesy of Rebecca Louise Law (photographer: Fe Norman); pp. 246–7 courtesy of Rebecca Louise Law; pp. 248–9 & portrait p. 286 courtesy of Rebecca Louise Law, photographer Nicola Tree (www.nicolatree.com).

Sara Johansson: all photos by Daniel Lindberg (www.gudali.se/www.gudali.wordpress.com).

Sarah Winward/Honey of a Thousand Flowers: pp. 257, 262, 263 & portrait p. 286 by Leo Patrone (www.leopatronephotography.com); pp. 258, 259 & 260–61 courtesy of Sarah Winward, Honey of a Thousand Flowers.

Saskia de Valk/Vlinder&Vogel: p. 264 courtesy of Saskia de Valk, Vlinder&Vogel; pp. 265, 268, 269 & portrait p. 286 by Studio Mirella Sahetapy (www.mirellasahetapy.com); pp. 266 & 267 by Jitske Hagens (www.wijzijnkees.nl).

Sean Cook/Mr.COOK: all photos by Andrew Lehmann (www.andrewlehmann.com).

Tracey Deep/Floral Sculptures: all photos by Nicholas Watt (www.nicholaswatt.com).

p. 288 Photo Kimberly Geneviève (www.kimberlygenevieve.com).

ACKNOWLEDGMENTS

The floral designers featured in this book are all composers, who demonstrate – in arrangement after arrangement – that it takes great talent to make even more stunning that which Nature readily offers. Match that with the perspective of a graphic designer, Bianca Wendt, who has embraced the concept of the project perfectly, and you have a book that is visually mesmerizing. I cannot thank the participants enough for their enthusiastic collaboration; my publishers and the people who have helped me throughout for their availability; and ultimately Mother Nature for being such a source of gifts that keep on giving.

ABOUT THE AUTHOR

Olivier Dupon is an expert in the fields of lifestyle and fashion, having begun his career at Christian Dior and worked as a buyer and project manager for several large retail companies before running his own boutique for several years. Based in Australia, he now scouts international markets in search of design/art/craft objects to feature on his blog, www.Dossier37.tumblr.com. His previous books are *The New Artisans* (published by Thames & Hudson in 2011), *The New Jewelers* (2012) and *The New Pâtissiers* (2013). A sequel to *The New Artisans* will be published in 2015.

On the cover: "Drying Roses", 2011, an art piece created for The Baltic, Southwark, London (www.balticrestaurant.co.uk). Courtesy of Rebecca Louise Law (see pp. 244–9).

First published in the United Kingdom in 2014 by Thames & Hudson Ltd, 181A High Holborn, London WC1V 7QX

Floral Contemporary © 2014 Olivier Dupon

Designed by Bianca Wendt Studio

British Library Cataloguing-in-Publication Data
A catalogue record for this book is available from the British Library

ISBN 978-0-500-51743-7

Printed and bound in China by C & C Offset Printing Co. Ltd

To find out about all our publications, please visit **www.thamesandhudson.com**. There you can subscribe to our e-newsletter, browse or download our current catalogue, and buy any titles that are in print.

Single rose detail from a photo shoot by Kristen Caissie of Moon Canyon Design (see pp. 176–83).